AF291599

Editor
Pamela Johnston

Designer
Nadine Rinderer

Editorial assistants
Clare Barrett, Rosa Ainley

Illustrations
All photos of JP's sculptures are by Sue Barr, except
for those on pp. 33, 53, 54, 60-61 and 74-75, which are
by Arthur Pickering.

ISBN 1 902902 37 8
978 1 902902 37 1

Colour separation and printing by SC (Sang Choy)
International Pte Ltd.

A catalogue of AA Publications is available from
36 Bedford Square, London WC1B 3ES
t + 44 (0)20 7887 4021 f + 44 (0)20 7414 0782
publications@aaschool.ac.uk
aaschool.ac.uk/publications

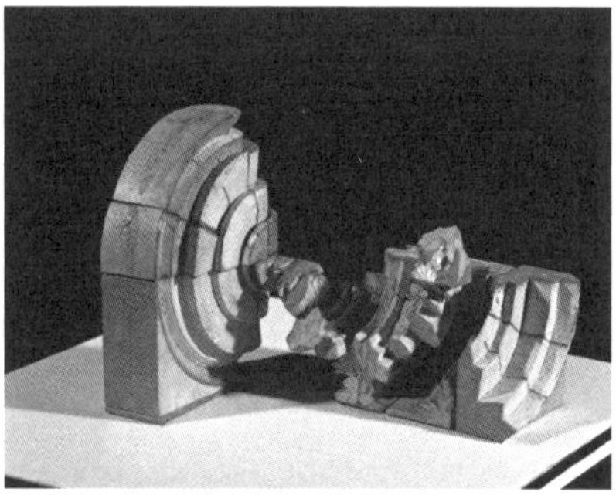

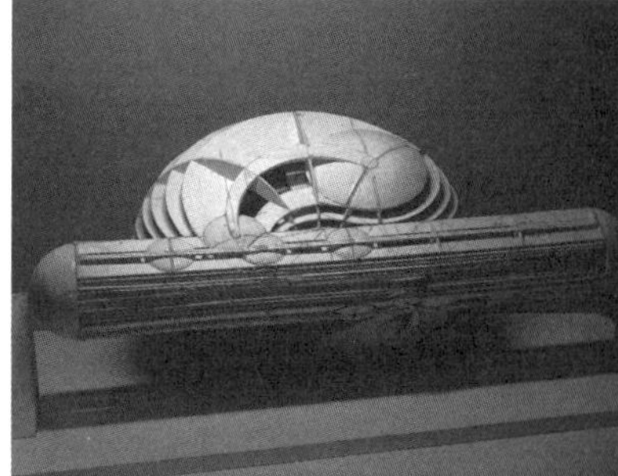

1965

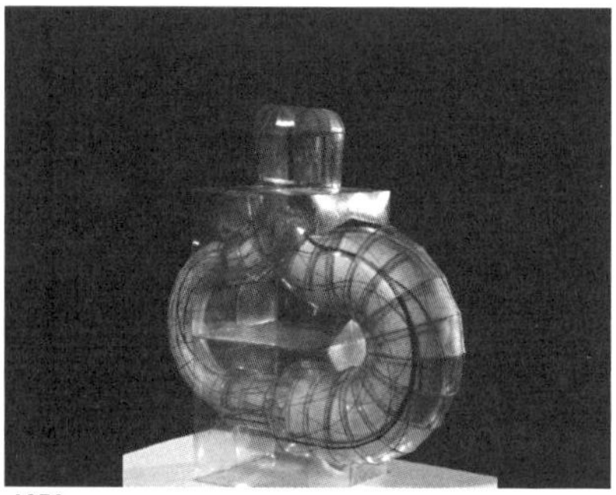

1970

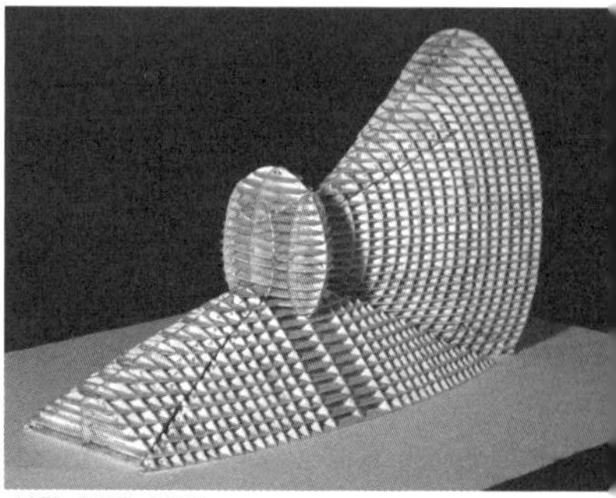

1971–1972–1973

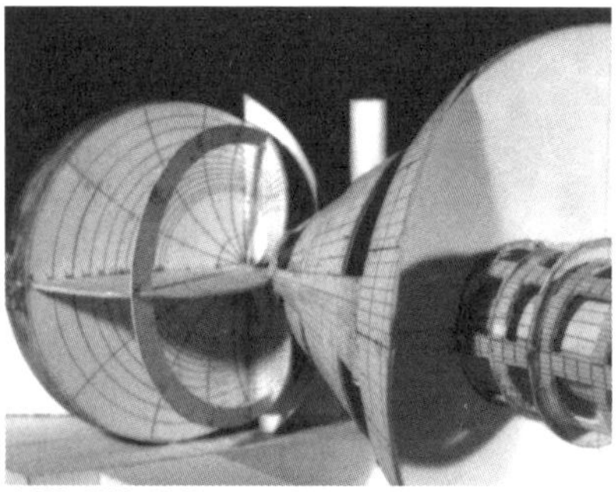

1978–1980–1981

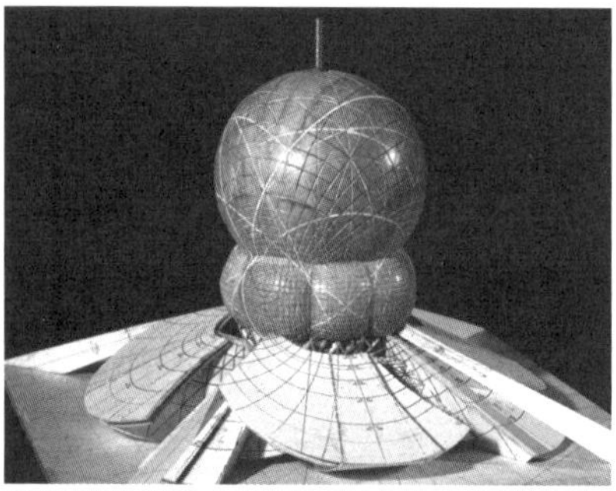

1981–1983–1984

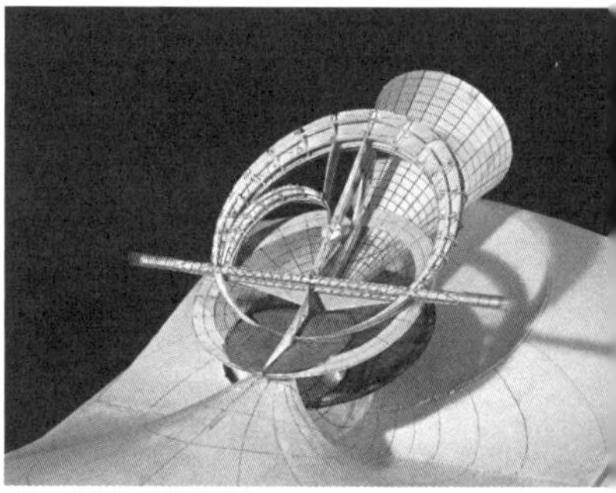

AUG 1987–APR 1988

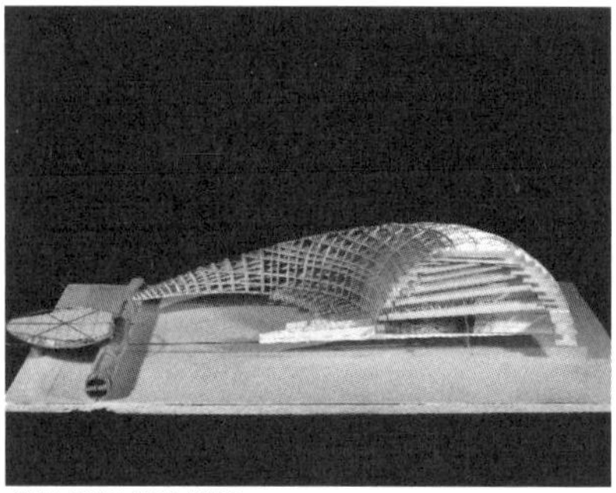

SEP 1990–APR 1992

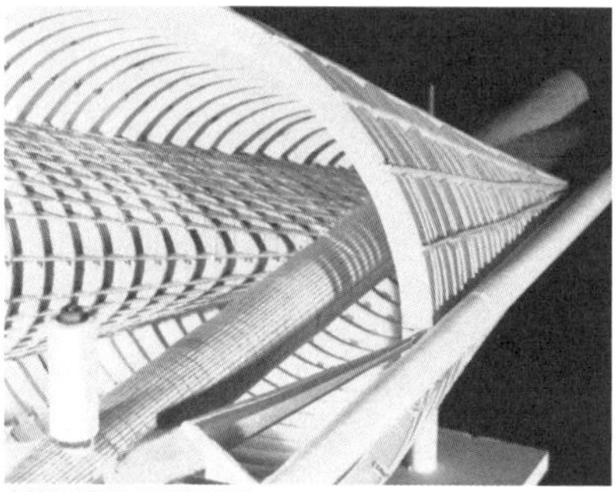

MAY 1992–DEC 1995

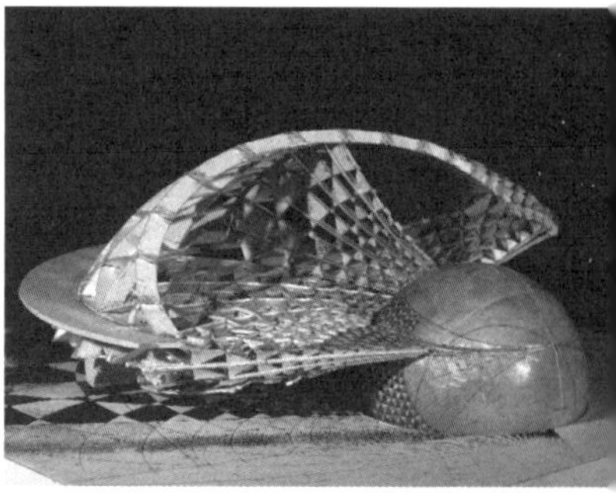

MAR 1996–SEP 1998

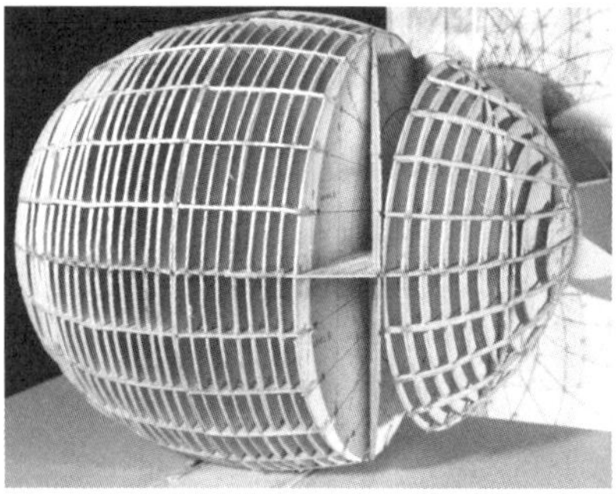

FEB–APR 2002

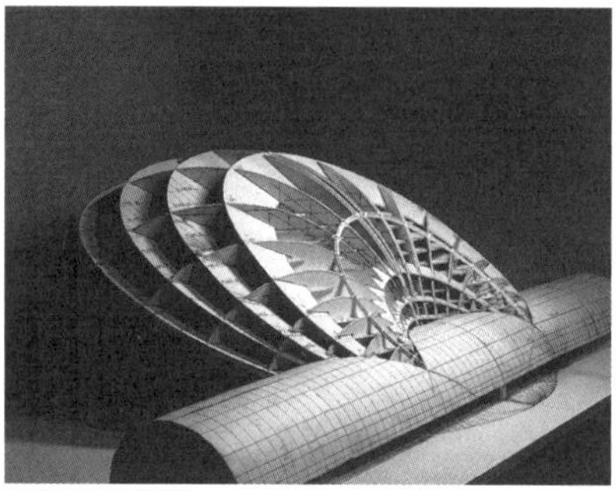

APR–OCT 2002

OCT–DEC 2002

Chronological development of
John Pickering's sculptures.

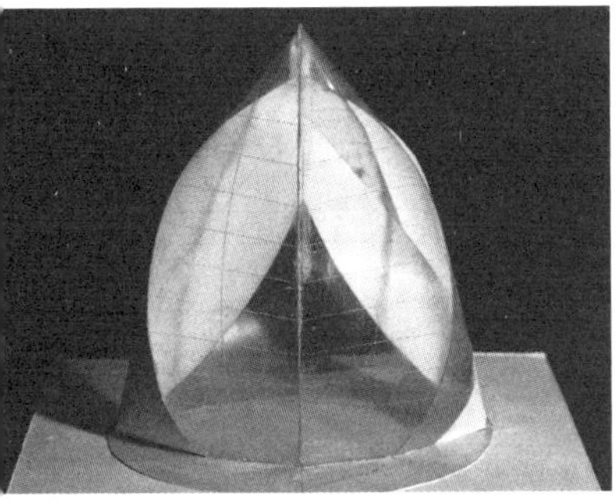

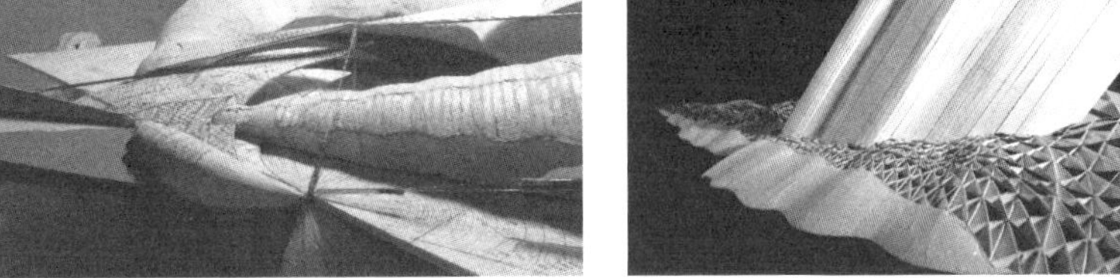

1973

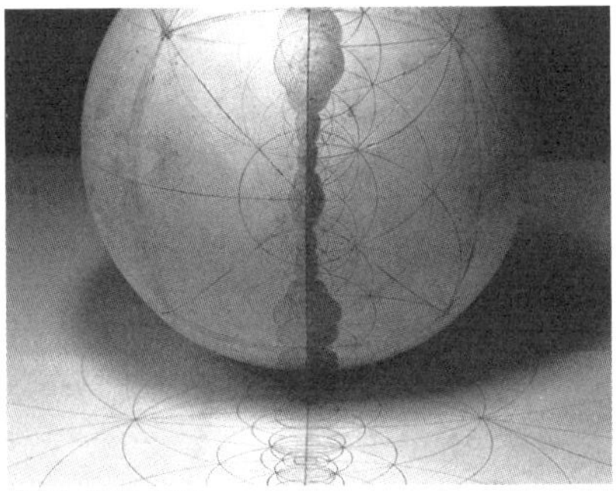

1973–1975–1976

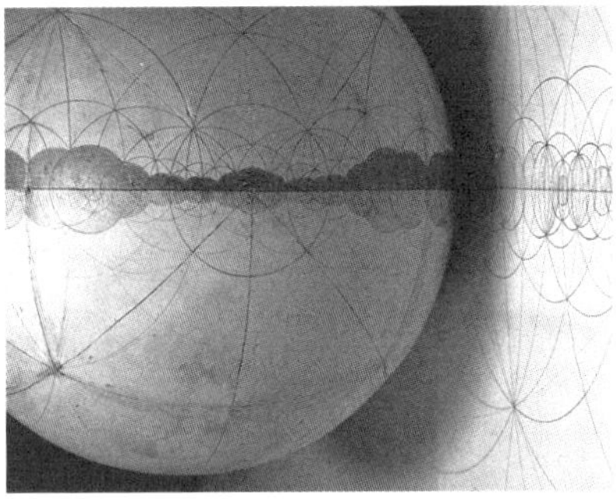

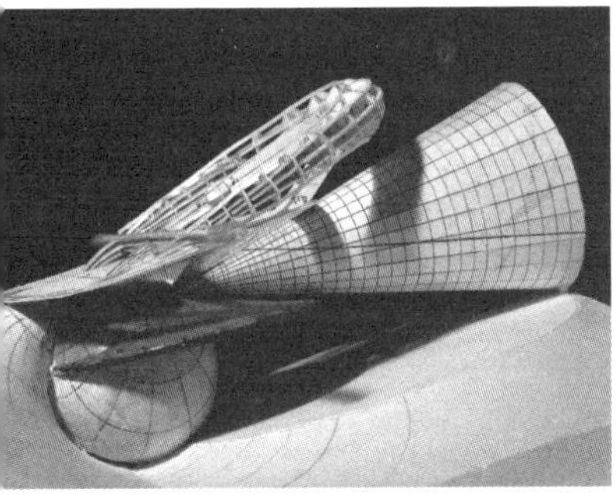

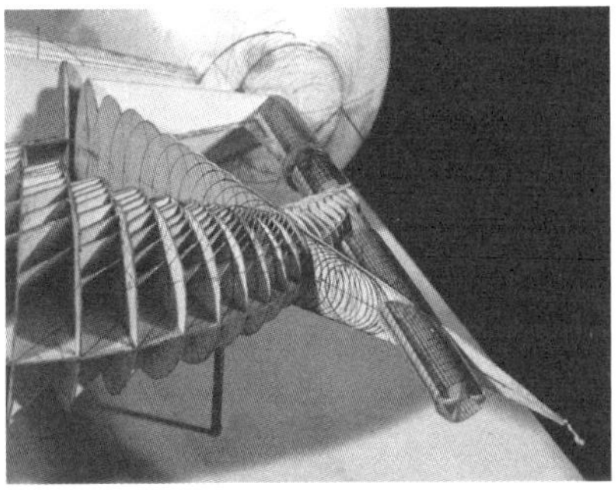

JUN 1988–AUG 1990

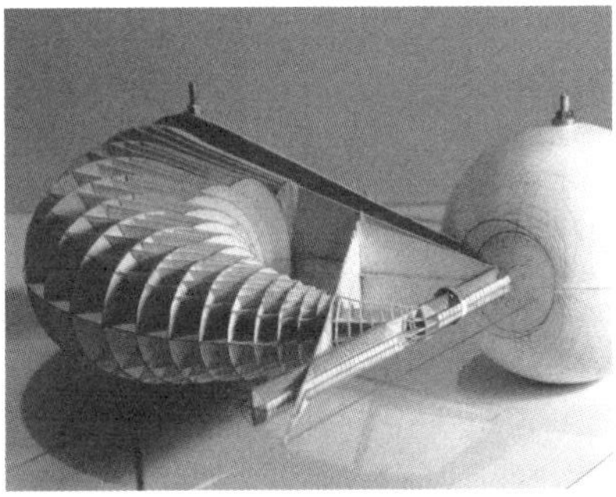

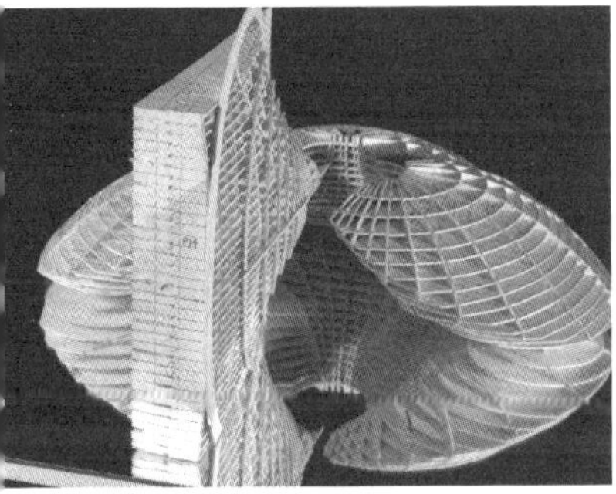

NOV 1998–JAN 2002

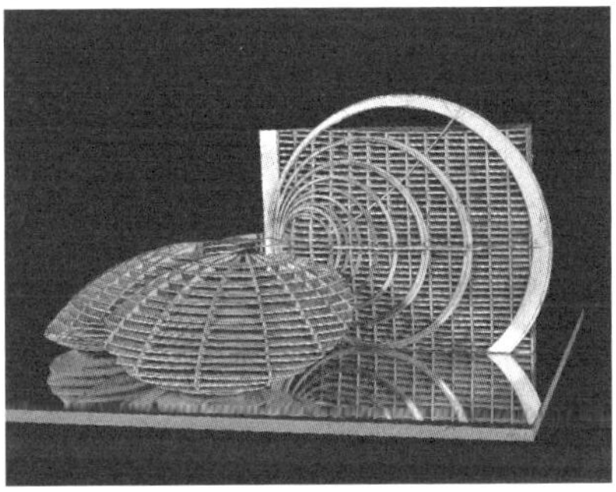

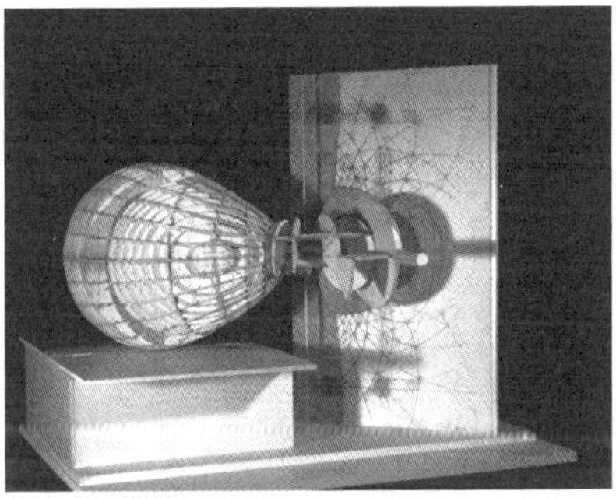

FEB–APR 2002

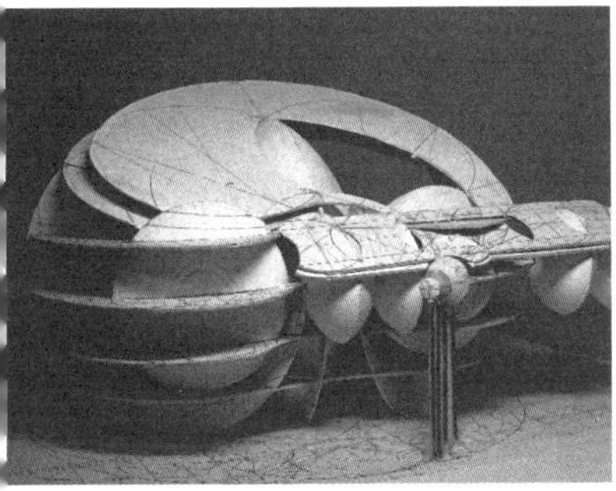

FEB 2003–OCT 2005

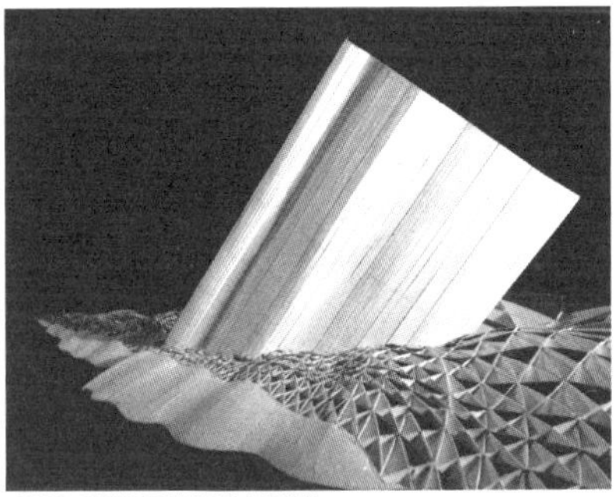

2006–WORK IN PROGRESS

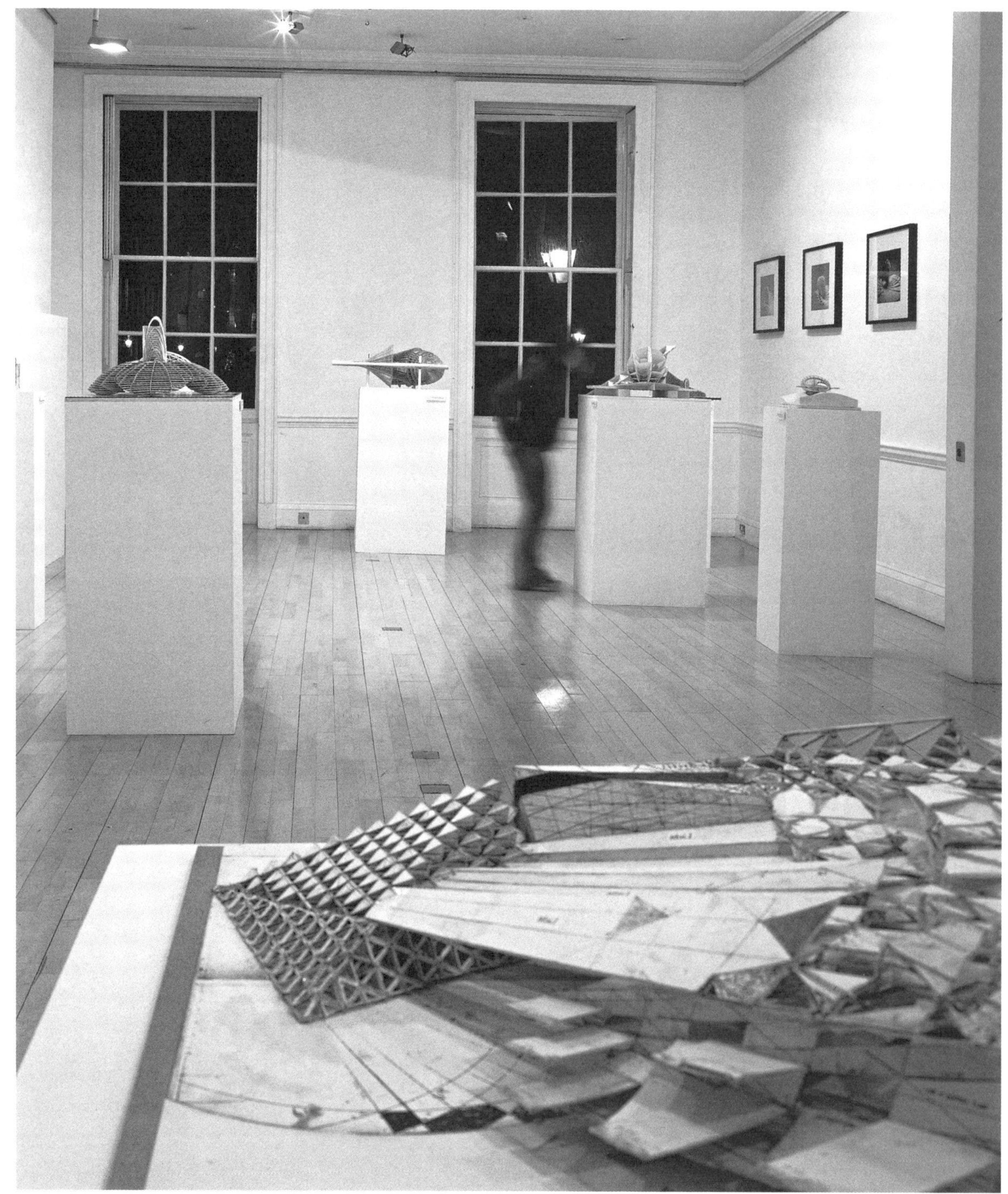

The Inversion Principle exhibition held in the AA Gallery,
November–December 2002.

'So I became anti-nature...'
One day John Pickering suddenly turned his back on the figurative drawings of his early years, when he loved the sound of running water – of a brook coursing over stones – and drew the curtains and left nature behind. 'So', he says with infectious laughter, 'I became anti-nature'. But despite this emphatic claim Pickering's fascination with geometry, inversion and fractals seems part of a ploy to get closer to nature. He stands in front of one of his pieces and imagines it as a large built structure, 'perhaps in Spain', he says, 'near the coast'.

Pickering's constructions are in many ways models, prototypes of giant structures waiting to be realised. In this sense his work shares many qualities with the various strands of utopian thinking in architecture and engineering that emphasise the symbolic and spatial qualities of structures rather than their purposive or functional dimensions. But while his sculptures may bear a resemblance to works of architecture, their origins are mathematical, and inasmuch as they are based on the variables of an equation they are (at least to begin with) non-visual.

This condition of non-visuality eventually gives way to a shift from the two-dimensional to the three-dimensional, when Pickering applies his eye to the assembly of artefacts that are not just mathematical but also compositional and associative. These constructions, without wishing to be illustrative, also make connections with the world of art, such as Mantegna's *Martyrdom of St Sebastian*, with the surfaces and textures of a body clearly in pain – something John Pickering, through his long-standing struggle with rheumatoid arthritis, must know a great deal about.

Pickering's hands are fragile yet they endure the slow and methodical process of turning the numerical data of an equation into form. He always maintains that it is the use of mathematics which gives him the freedom to organise his constructions as well as to choose what to leave out. The process echoes the 'statistical compositions' of Karlheinz Stockhausen, one of Pickering's favourite composers. And the results – these curved and figurative movements of mathematical form – provide a heroic counterpoint to the prevalent digital imagery born of speed. Unlike the seemingly instantaneous becoming of digital surfaces, Pickering's constructions reveal the traces of their gradual shift to the three-dimensional. At once precise and to scale as objects, yet a-scalar as spatial structures, they wait to be inhabited by our imaginations.

Mohsen Mostafavi

JP'S WAY

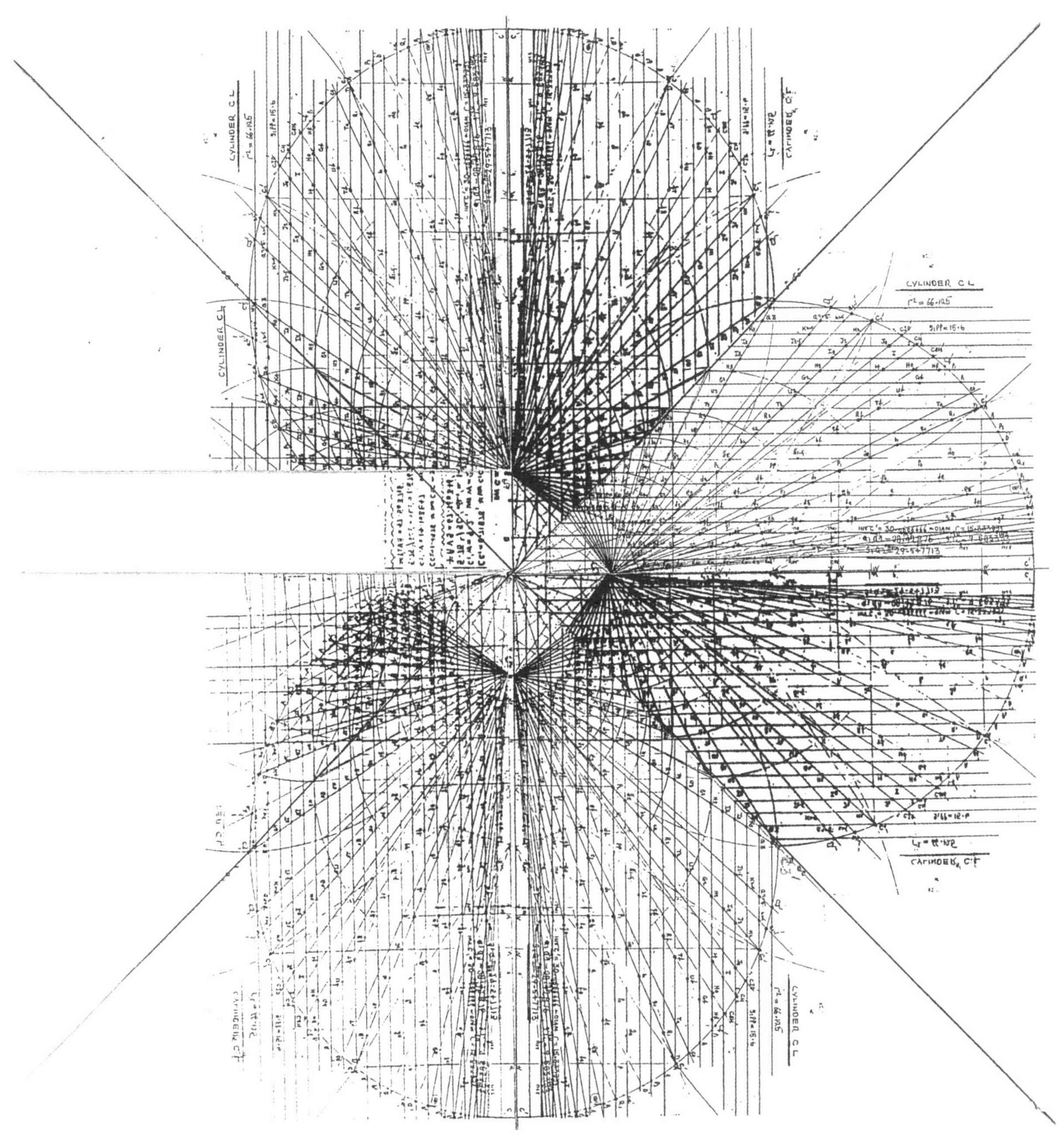

Inverting a cylinder CL with respect to a point not lying on
the cylinder. The resulting cylinder is subject to reflection
and rotation, therefore three cyclides intersect one another.
See pp. 36-37 for model view.

JP's Way

John Pickering (JP for short) is a British artist who uses mathematics to produce small, finely wrought sculptures brimming with architectonic qualities. From the large body of algebra available to the lover of visual maths, JP borrows one equation only. His chosen equation describes a two-dimensional transformation called *inversion,* which involves a wholesale reflection of figures about a circle. As explained in detail by the mathematician John Sharp in the appended essay on the technical implications of JP's art, inversion consists in *mapping* – or drawing metric correspondences between – separate points across the circumference of a circle. The mapping of points can be easily generalised to the mapping of curves and all simple kinds of geometric figure (also known as primitives), be they two-dimensional or three-dimensional. JP methodically applies the principles of inversion to various primitives (spheres, cylinders, cones, cross-caps and so on) and explores the striking manifestations of their transformation in space. His chosen tactics for putting sculptures together require the use of dozens of two-dimensional cut-out profiles. This is partly down to JP's choice of a two-dimensional transformation, and partly down to his intuition as a sculptor. As the writer and engineer Chris Wise reminds us in his essay 'John Pickering: Perfect Imperfect', JP's material embodiments of mathematical surfaces are always indirect: JP does not show the surface itself as it were, only a negative imprint of it (more like a mould), which viewers are invited to visualise in their own terms. For the record, the manual calculation, drawing, cutting and gluing of the cut-outs as practised by JP are highly labour-intensive, a perplexing choice compounded by the artist's impaired motor abilities (JP suffers from a degenerative condition that hampers the use of his hands). Finally, JP regards the *process* of applying the rules of inversion as equally important for the aesthetic worth of the sculpture produced: untypically for an artist, he communicates in detail the steps he has taken to get to the final result. In any case the sheer beauty and material sophistication of his sculpture, which involves card-cutting and plaster-casting, cannot be accounted for on the basis of mathematics alone.

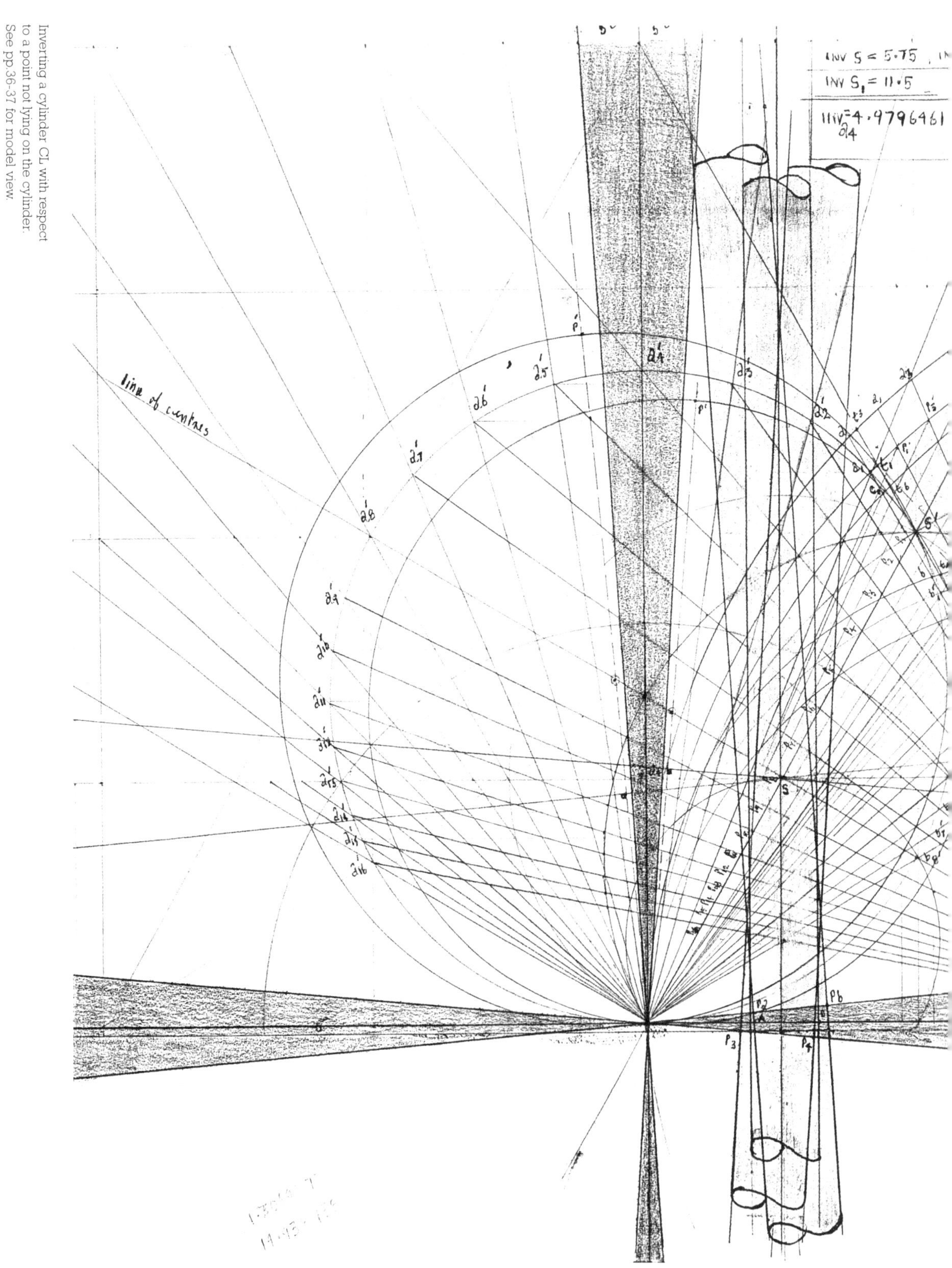

Inverting a cylinder CL with respect to a point not lying on the cylinder. See pp.36-37 for model view.

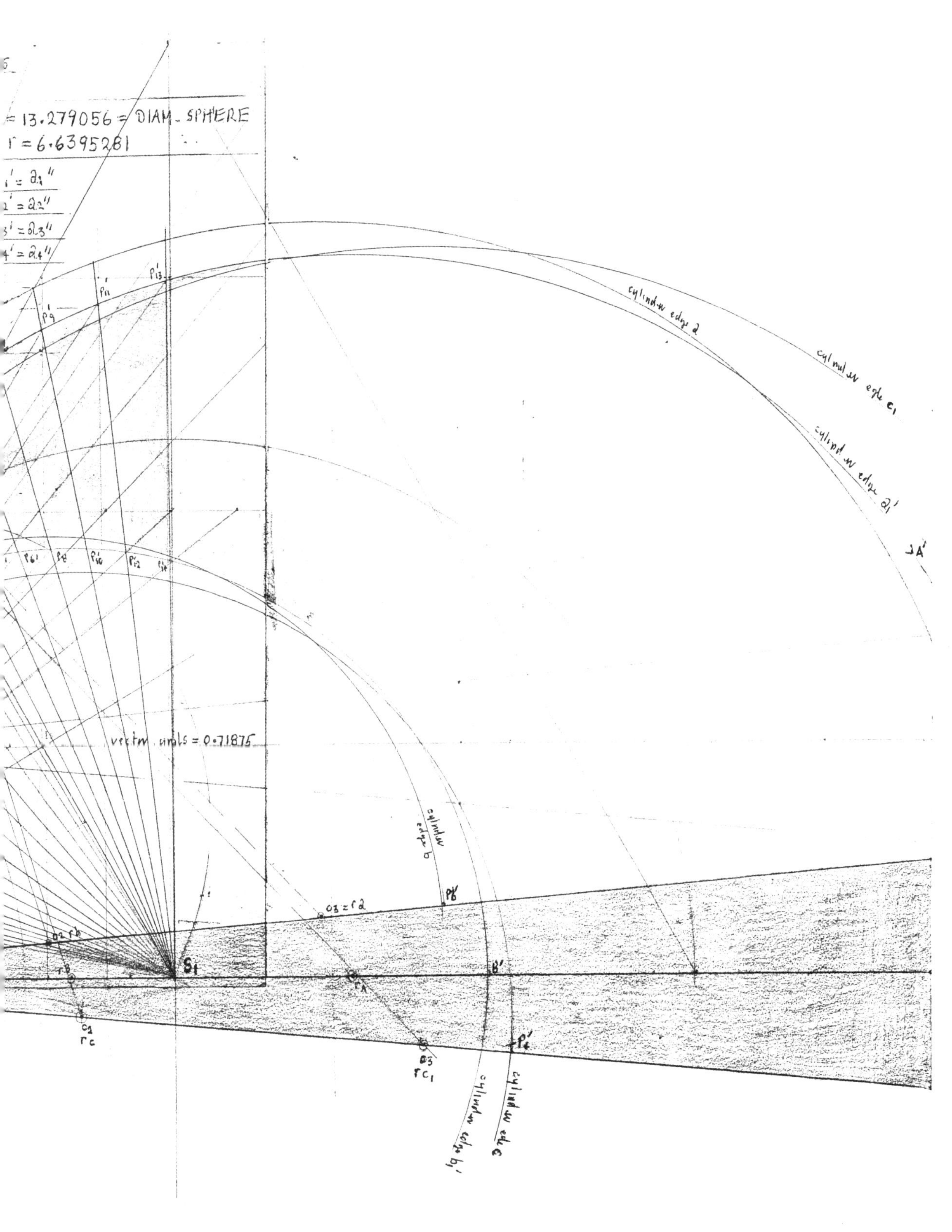
= 13.279056 = DIAM. SPHERE
r = 6.6395281
vector angles = 0.71875
cylinder edge d
cylinder edge e₁
cylinder edge d₁
cylinder edge b
cylinder edge b₁
cylinder edge e
S₁
o₃ = r2
o₂ = r b
o₁ rc
rb

This brief summary introduces some of the issues dealt with in greater detail by Chris Wise and John Sharp in their respective contributions to the critical assessment of the artist's work. The remainder of the essay is solely intended as an architect's response to some questions raised by JP's work, considered against the backdrop of an architectural profession dominated by the proliferation of computer modelling technologies, the increased pursuit of mathematical and biomorphic models of form, and the wholesale identification of a fringe of the profession with the ambitions of mathematicians and scientists in general (the other two essays in the book touch on this too).

The key question here is not so much whether the inversion principle produces architecture (it does, and at the same time it doesn't), but the extent to which JP's sculptural art can help us refine our understanding of architecture's own disciplinary goals. As the very existence of this publication attests, the discipline of architecture has promptly embraced JP's life-work, much more so than the art world, to which it nominally belongs. There are at least two good reasons for this: JP's sculpture displays the same qualities as architecture (it is overtly rational, process-oriented, and given to tectonic expression), and it is also subject to the same limitations, weaknesses and pitfalls as architecture (a matter to be elaborated on further). JP's abstract sculptures can be all at once *more* architectural and *less* architectural than many 'literal' building proposals, though never predictably so.

JP's way is fundamentally interdisciplinary, and that is its strength. It is all at once fabrication and surface engineering (in a proto sort of way), as well as sculpture and material expression; it is architectonics, as well as visual art, and applied mathematics. His work does many things, but from the vantage point of the architectural critic it is better to describe it in terms of what it *does not do.* For all its interdisciplinary affinities, the unique character of JP's way can be seen through the prism of the following *oppositions:* it is model-based rather than drawn, two-dimensional rather than three-dimensional, analytic rather than descriptive, figurative rather than abstract, process-based rather than product-orientated (as well as the other way around), compositional rather than transformation-based (and vice versa), and slow and manual rather than fast and mechanised. The scope of each assertion is not as clear-cut as the list suggests, but each says something essential about the nature of JP's intriguing work while bringing it within closer range of – or drawing it further afield from – the disciplinary boundaries of architecture. Let us examine these statements one by one.

JP's way is model-based rather than drawn. He works primarily in two dimensions, but seldom draws. The diagrams produced in support of his process resolve the technical hurdles of
inverting figures and curves, but they are not *representational* in
a traditional sense: they do not depict the final object, or they do
so only in part, and without the graphic clarity and standard use
of convention associated with architectural and engineering
drawing. The latter would be redundant anyway. Insofar as JP
calculates a form by analytic means, he does not need to draw it
in order to see it and make decisions, and in this his art is clearly
unlike architecture. What is it like then? JP's ultimate output is a
model. That is a significant fact in itself. Since the model is of
a rather modest scale, one hesitates to call his art 'building',
although it is not 'model-making' either, because there is no
given blueprint to work to. Typically, an architect will hand out
a ready-made blueprint of a form to the model-maker, who
executes it faithfully. In JP's work the blueprint and the physical
model of the form are developed at the same time: as a matter
of fact they are one and the same thing. And insofar as there *is*
a blueprint to JP's creations (and a technically elaborate one, as
he likes to remind us), one hesitates to simply call them 'sculptures' either. Thus JP's work exists in a sort of disciplinary gap,
where the instrumental premises of architecture, sculpture,
building and engineering meet and cancel each other out.

JP's way is two-dimensional, rather than three-dimensional.
Inversion is a two-dimensional transformation, and JP's form-
giving process consists in calculating and cutting out two-
See illustration
overleaf.
dimensional profiles before piecing together a three-dimensional object out of them. While the mathematician may see an
unnecessary detour here, from the vantage point of the architect
there is no detour at all: inasmuch as it takes the form of drawing
rather than building, *the work of the architect is always two-
dimensional*: it expresses itself as plan and section (or any deri-
vation thereof), two diagrams which reduce the complexity of
space into planes (the modalities of this reduction have been
refined over a four-hundred-year period and are still in flux).
With the advent of modelling software, the elaboration of form
increasingly takes place directly in three dimensions, but these
computer-generated forms may not be drawn or built rationally
without being reduced in some way or other (by projection,
triangulation, development or flattening) back to the two-dimensional medium of the architect. Structural engineers refer to this
process as 'rationalising a form'. JP's emphasis on beginning
with two-dimensional profiles means that he chooses to pre-
rationalise the construction of complex three-dimensional forms,

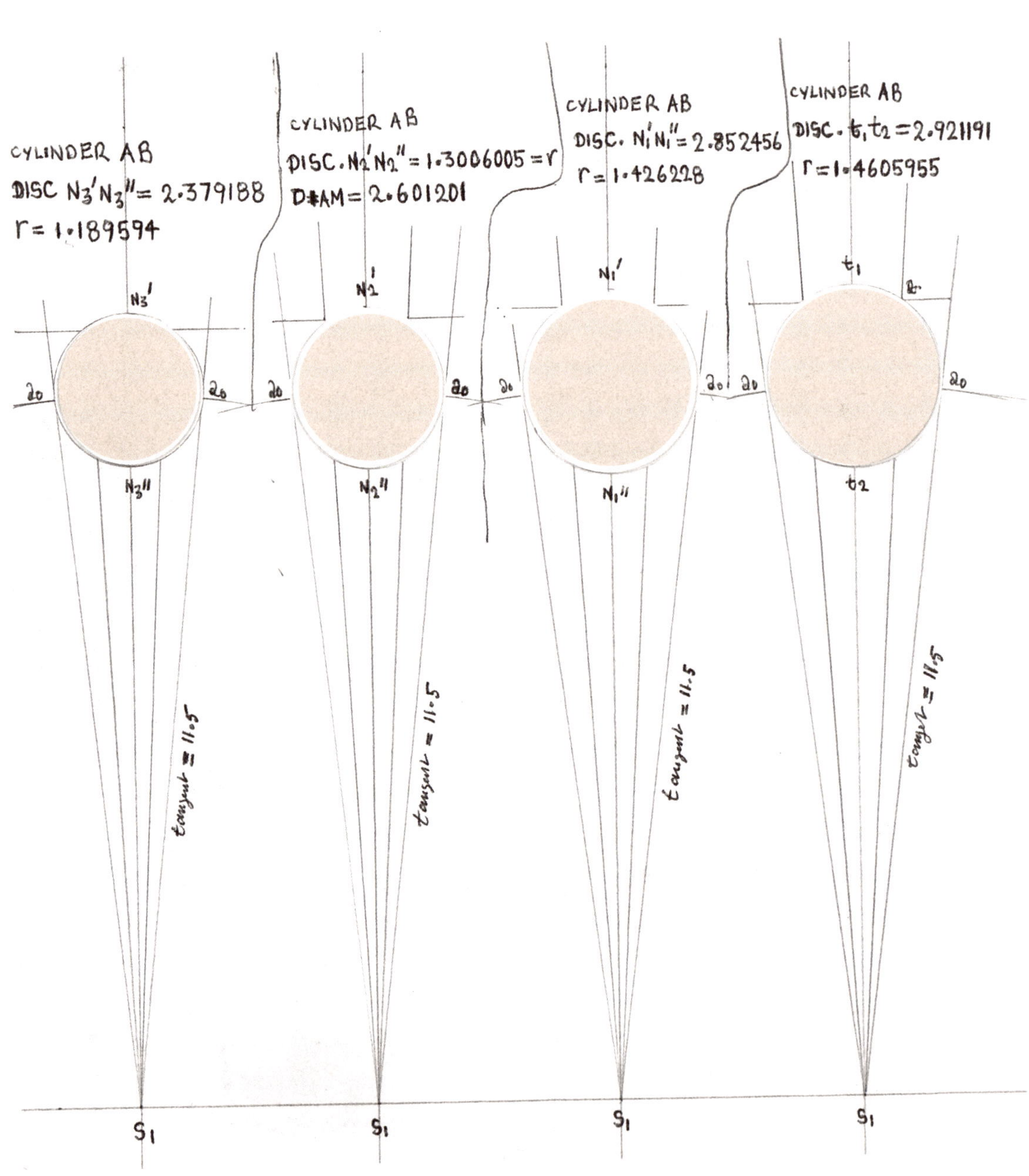

Inverting a cylinder AB where the centre of inversion does not lie on the cylinder, cut-out profiles. See pp. 52-53 for model views.

something he has in common with all good engineers. Most importantly, by working as it were in two dimensions only, JP adheres to the instrumental premises (and limitations) of architecture proper. Often he is even several steps ahead of those architects who do not wish to understand the geometric make-up of the 3D forms they devise on the computer and routinely give them up for *post-rationalisation*, with all the attendant loss of control over their eventual material translation.

JP understands the three-dimensional surface primarily in analytic terms. To define his forms he resorts to algebra and analytic geometry, rather than Euclidean geometry. To put it another way, rather than graphically manipulating points and lines, he uses numbers and symbolic operators. To be sure, since the inversion principle is an application of projective geometry, JP does draw a lot of figures, but they play an auxiliary role in the process of discovery; they are more visual mementos and illustrations of numerical calculations than operative means of developing a form. JP needs them primarily to *index* (or locate in space) the hundreds of distance measurements and subsequent calculations that his chosen method requires, and these calculations are the real engine of the process. They fill out whole pages of his notebooks. Sometimes their visual density reminds us of the numeric matter produced by *file output streams* (the strings of numbers generated by a computer application), were it not for the perky line, the occasional erasure and the child-like application of the writing, all of which betray JP's distinctive hand and endow his technique with a personal 'touch' (JP reports all his calculations manually on the sheet).

See illustration overleaf.

To my knowledge there are no contemporary precedents of architects using analytic and projective geometry in this way: JP operates in a sort of void. Some precedents come to mind from the seventeenth and eighteenth centuries (when the discipline of geometry underwent a theoretical consolidation), but the architects who used projective geometry left no systematic record of their working process – much like those of us today who opt to pursue this tradition with the help of modelling software (unlike our forebears, however, we do not understand mathematics).

<u>CONE INV q12 h12 $r_2 = 66.125$</u>

vector length

INV. q12 = 34.619584 ÷ 12

INV P_1 = 2.8849653	INV P_1' = 22.920553
INV P_2 = 5.7699307	INV P_2' = 11.460276
INV P_3 = 8.654896	INV P_3' = 7.6401842
INV P_4 = 11.539861	INV P_4' = 5.7301383
INV P_5 = 14.424827	INV P_5' = 4.5841104
INV P_6 = 17.309792	INV P_6' = 3.8200921
INV P_7 = 20.194757	INV P_7' = 3.2743647
INV P_8 = 23.079723	INV P_8' = 2.8650691
INV P_9 = 25.964688	INV P_9' = 2.5467281
INV P_{10} = 28.849653	INV P_{10}' = 2.2920553
INV P_{11} = 31.734618	INV P_{11}' = 2.0836867
INV P_{12} = 34.619584	INV P_{12}' = 1.9100461

VECTOR LENGTH

INV 15° = 34.635851 ÷ 12

INV P_1 = 2.8863209	INV P_1' = 22.909788
INV P_2 = 5.7726418	INV P_2' = 11.454894
INV P_3 = 8.6589628	INV P_3' = 7.6365959
INV P_4 = 11.545284	INV P_4' = 5.7274468
INV P_5 = 14.431605	INV P_5' = 4.5819575
INV P_6 = 17.317925	INV P_6' = 3.8182981
INV P_7 = 20.204246	INV P_7' = 3.2728269
INV P_8 = 23.090567	INV P_8' = 2.8637235
INV P_9 = 25.976888	INV P_9' = 2.545532
INV P_{10} = 28.863209	INV P_{10}' = 2.2909788
INV P_{11} = 31.74953	INV P_{11}' = 2.082708
INV P_{12} = 34.635851	INV P_{12}' = 1.909149

VECTOR LENGTH

INV 30° = 34.683499 ÷ 12

INV P_1 = 2.8902916	INV P_1' = 22.878314
INV P_2 = 5.7805832	INV P_2' = 11.439157
INV P_3 = 8.6708747	INV P_3' = 7.6261049
INV P_4 = 11.561166	INV P_4' = 5.7195788
INV P_5 = 14.451458	INV P_5' = 4.5756629
INV P_6 = 17.341749	INV P_6' = 3.8130525
INV P_7 = 20.232041	INV P_7' = 3.2683307
INV P_8 = 23.122332	INV P_8' = 2.8597894
INV P_9 = 26.012624	INV P_9' = 2.542035
INV P_{10} = 28.902915	INV P_{10}' = 2.2878315
INV P_{11} = 31.793207	INV P_{11}' = 2.0798468
INV P_{12} = 34.683498	INV P_{12}' = 1.9065263

VECTOR LENGTH

INV 45° = 34.759163 ÷ 12

INV P_1 = 2.8965969	INV P_1' = 22.828513
INV P_2 = 5.7931938	INV P_2' = 11.414257
INV P_3 = 8.6897908	INV P_3' = 7.6095043
INV P_4 = 11.586388	INV P_4' = 5.7071281
INV P_5 = 14.482985	INV P_5' = 4.5657024
INV P_6 = 17.379581	INV P_6' = 3.8047523
INV P_7 = 20.276178	INV P_7' = 3.2612162
INV P_8 = 23.172775	INV P_8' = 2.8535642
INV P_9 = 26.069372	INV P_9' = 2.5365015
INV P_{10} = 28.965969	INV P_{10}' = 2.2828513
INV P_{11} = 31.862566	INV P_{11}' = 2.0753194
INV P_{12} = 34.759163	INV P_{12}' = 1.9023761

VECTOR LENGTH

INV 60° = 34.857522

INV P_1 = 2.9047935	INV P_1' = 22.764097
INV P_2 = 5.809587	INV P_2' = 11.382048
INV P_3 = 8.7143805	INV P_3' = 7.5880322
INV P_4 = 11.619174	INV P_4' = 5.6910242
INV P_5 = 14.523968	INV P_5' = 4.5528192
INV P_6 = 17.428761	INV P_6' = 3.7940161
INV P_7 = 20.333555	INV P_7' = 3.2520137
INV P_8 = 23.238348	INV P_8' = 2.8455121
INV P_9 = 26.143142	INV P_9' = 2.529344
INV P_{10} = 29.047935	INV P_{10}' = 2.2764097
INV P_{11} = 31.952729	INV P_{11}' = 2.0694633
INV P_{12} = 34.857522	INV P_{12}' = 1.8970081

VECTOR LENGTH

INV 75° = 34.971716 ÷ 12

INV P_1 = 2.9143097	INV P_1' = 22.689764
INV P_2 = 5.8286193	INV P_2' = 11.344882
INV P_3 = 8.742929	INV P_3' = 7.5632548
INV P_4 = 11.657239	INV P_4' = 5.672441
INV P_5 = 14.571548	INV P_5' = 4.537953
INV P_6 = 17.485858	INV P_6' = 3.7816274
INV P_7 = 20.400167	INV P_7' = 3.241395
INV P_8 = 23.314477	INV P_8' = 2.8362206
INV P_9 = 26.228787	INV P_9' = 2.5210849
INV P_{10} = 29.143096	INV P_{10}' = 2.2689765
INV P_{11} = 32.057406	INV P_{11}' = 2.0627059
INV P_{12} = 34.971715	INV P_{12}' = 1.8908138

CONE INV q_{12} h_{12} $r^2 = 66 \cdot 125$

VECTOR LENGTH
INV $90° = 35 \cdot 093847 \div 12$

INV $P_1 = 2 \cdot 9244873$	INV $P_1' = 22 \cdot 610801$
INV $P_2 = 5 \cdot 8489745$	INV $P_2' = 11 \cdot 305401$
INV $P_3 = 8 \cdot 7734618$	INV $P_3' = 7 \cdot 5369337$
INV $P_4 = 11 \cdot 697949$	INV $P_4' = 5 \cdot 6527003$
INV $P_5 = 14 \cdot 622436$	INV $P_5' = 4 \cdot 5221603$
INV $P_6 = 17 \cdot 546923$	INV $P_6' = 3 \cdot 768467$
INV $P_7 = 20 \cdot 471411$	INV $P_7' = 3 \cdot 2301144$
INV $P_8 = 23 \cdot 395898$	INV $P_8' = 2 \cdot 8263502$
INV $P_9 = 26 \cdot 320385$	INV $P_9' = 2 \cdot 5123113$
INV $P_{10} = 29 \cdot 244872$	INV $P_{10}' = 2 \cdot 2610802$
INV $P_{11} = 32 \cdot 169359$	INV $P_{11}' = 2 \cdot 0555274$
INV $P_{12} = 35 \cdot 093847$	INV $P_{12}' = 1 \cdot 8842334$

VECTOR LENGTH
INV $105° = 35 \cdot 215555 \div 12$

INV $P_1 = 2 \cdot 9346296$	INV $P_1' = 22 \cdot 532656$
INV $P_2 = 5 \cdot 8692592$	INV $P_2' = 11 \cdot 266328$
INV $P_3 = 8 \cdot 8038887$	INV $P_3' = 7 \cdot 5108855$
INV $P_4 = 11 \cdot 738518$	INV $P_4' = 5 \cdot 6331643$
INV $P_5 = 14 \cdot 673148$	INV $P_5' = 4 \cdot 5065313$
INV $P_6 = 17 \cdot 607777$	INV $P_6' = 3 \cdot 7554428$
INV $P_7 = 20 \cdot 542407$	INV $P_7' = 3 \cdot 2189509$
INV $P_8 = 23 \cdot 477036$	INV $P_8' = 2 \cdot 8165821$
INV $P_9 = 26 \cdot 411666$	INV $P_9' = 2 \cdot 5036285$
INV $P_{10} = 29 \cdot 346295$	INV $P_{10}' = 2 \cdot 2532657$
INV $P_{11} = 32 \cdot 280925$	INV $P_{11}' = 2 \cdot 0484233$
INV $P_{12} = 35 \cdot 215554$	INV $P_{12}' = 1 \cdot 8777214$

VECTOR LENGTH
INV $120° = 35 \cdot 328592 \div 12$

INV $P_1 = 2 \cdot 9440493$	INV $P_1' = 22 \cdot 460561$
INV $P_2 = 5 \cdot 8880987$	INV $P_2' = 11 \cdot 230281$
INV $P_3 = 8 \cdot 832148$	INV $P_3' = 7 \cdot 4868537$
INV $P_4 = 11 \cdot 776197$	INV $P_4' = 5 \cdot 6151404$
INV $P_5 = 14 \cdot 720247$	INV $P_5' = 4 \cdot 4921121$
INV $P_6 = 17 \cdot 664296$	INV $P_6' = 3 \cdot 7434269$
INV $P_7 = 20 \cdot 608345$	INV $P_7' = 3 \cdot 2086516$
INV $P_8 = 23 \cdot 552395$	INV $P_8' = 2 \cdot 8075701$
INV $P_9 = 26 \cdot 496444$	INV $P_9' = 2 \cdot 4956179$
INV $P_{10} = 29 \cdot 440493$	INV $P_{10}' = 2 \cdot 2460561$
INV $P_{11} = 32 \cdot 384542$	INV $P_{11}' = 2 \cdot 0418692$
INV $P_{12} = 35 \cdot 328592$	INV $P_{12}' = 1 \cdot 8717134$

VECTOR LENGTH
INV $135° = 35 \cdot 42537 \div 12$

INV $P_1' = 2 \cdot 9521142$	INV $P_1' = 22 \cdot 399201$
INV $P_2' = 5 \cdot 9042283$	INV $P_2' = 11 \cdot 199601$
INV $P_3' = 8 \cdot 8563425$	INV $P_3' = 7 \cdot 4664005$
INV $P_4' = 11 \cdot 808457$	INV $P_4' = 5 \cdot 5998002$
INV $P_5' = 14 \cdot 760571$	INV $P_5' = 4 \cdot 4798402$
INV $P_6' = 17 \cdot 712685$	INV $P_6' = 3 \cdot 7332003$
INV $P_7' = 20 \cdot 664799$	INV $P_7' = 3 \cdot 199886$
INV $P_8' = 23 \cdot 616913$	INV $P_8' = 2 \cdot 7999002$
INV $P_9' = 26 \cdot 569027$	INV $P_9' = 2 \cdot 4888002$
INV $P_{10}' = 29 \cdot 521141$	INV $P_{10}' = 2 \cdot 2399202$
INV $P_{11}' = 32 \cdot 473255$	INV $P_{11}' = 2 \cdot 0362911$
INV $P_{12}' = 35 \cdot 425369$	INV $P_{12}' = 1 \cdot 8666001$

VECTOR LENGTH
INV $150° = 35 \cdot 499451 \div 12$

INV $P_1 = 2 \cdot 9582876$	INV $P_1' = 22 \cdot 352458$
INV $P_2 = 5 \cdot 9165752$	INV $P_2' = 11 \cdot 176229$
INV $P_3 = 8 \cdot 8748627$	INV $P_3' = 7 \cdot 4508195$
INV $P_4 = 11 \cdot 83315$	INV $P_4' = 5 \cdot 5881148$
INV $P_5 = 14 \cdot 791438$	INV $P_5' = 4 \cdot 470917$
INV $P_6 = 17 \cdot 749725$	INV $P_6' = 3 \cdot 7254098$
INV $P_7 = 20 \cdot 708013$	INV $P_7' = 3 \cdot 1932084$
INV $P_8 = 23 \cdot 6663$	INV $P_8' = 2 \cdot 7940574$
INV $P_9 = 26 \cdot 624588$	INV $P_9' = 2 \cdot 4836065$
INV $P_{10} = 29 \cdot 582875$	INV $P_{10}' = 2 \cdot 2352459$
INV $P_{11} = 32 \cdot 541163$	INV $P_{11}' = 2 \cdot 0320417$
INV $P_{12} = 35 \cdot 49945$	INV $P_{12}' = 1 \cdot 8627049$

VECTOR LENGTH
INV $165° = 35 \cdot 545943 \div 12$

INV $P_1 = 2 \cdot 9621619$	INV $P_1' = 22 \cdot 323223$
INV $P_2 = 5 \cdot 9243238$	INV $P_2' = 11 \cdot 161611$
INV $P_3 = 8 \cdot 8864858$	INV $P_3' = 7 \cdot 4410742$
INV $P_4 = 11 \cdot 848648$	INV $P_4' = 5 \cdot 5808055$
INV $P_5 = 14 \cdot 81081$	INV $P_5' = 4 \cdot 4646444$
INV $P_6 = 17 \cdot 772971$	INV $P_6' = 3 \cdot 7205372$
INV $P_7 = 20 \cdot 735133$	INV $P_7' = 3 \cdot 1890319$
INV $P_8 = 23 \cdot 697295$	INV $P_8' = 2 \cdot 7904029$
INV $P_9 = 26 \cdot 659457$	INV $P_9' = 2 \cdot 4803581$
INV $P_{10} = 29 \cdot 621619$	INV $P_{10}' = 2 \cdot 2323223$
INV $P_{11} = 32 \cdot 583781$	INV $P_{11}' = 2 \cdot 0293839$
INV $P_{12} = 35 \cdot 545943$	INV $P_{12}' = 1 \cdot 8602686$

Yet JP is not quite on his own. Recent examples of architects using another kind of foundational geometry abound, and the early work of Preston Scott Cohen leaps to mind. Contrary to JP's analytic approach, Cohen's brand of projective geometry relies exclusively on descriptive means, but his working ethos and technique bear an uncanny resemblance to JP's own. Comparing JP's *Inverting a cylinder CL with respect to a point not lying on the cylinder* with Cohen's *Stereotomic permutations*, we come to the following conclusions: both strategies involve the rigorous application of geometric rules; they are both carried out by hand and rely on the persistence of palimpsest-like accumulations of graphic matter, which crowd out the intended result and steer our attention firmly towards the process itself; and they are equally abstract in their architectural implications. But the similarities end there. The effect the work has on us varies sharply. Cohen's mystifying accumulation of lines keeps us in awe of the defunct but clearly recognisable tradition which begins with *Gaspard Monge* and *Gérard Desargues;* the sight of JP's notebooks, on the other hand, with their acres of handwritten numeric calculations, triggers a sense of disbelief, and perhaps a tinge of doubt. Among architects at least, an excessive concentration of symbols is more likely to summon fantasies of misapplied science than an excessive concentration of lines. This is only because of prejudice. Pound for pound the two strategies are equivalent, except that JP's work has no recognisable tradition to latch onto (the far more important historic breakthroughs in analytic geometry by Descartes, Newton, Fermat and Wallis, among others, are not as well known).

See drawings on pp. 10, 12 and 26 and model views on pp. 36-37.

JP's way is process-based, rather than product-orientated. Depending on the angle of consideration, it appears to be about the technical process whereby figures are inverted about a circle, and the endless subtleties of this inversion; equally, it appears to be about the presence of a material artefact, awesome and arresting in its own right. The two perceptions may well coexist, but where an ordinary artist would not suggest a particular reading of his or her own work, JP develops and communicates his art at two distinct levels: first, as mathematical generation, always explicitly articulated and fully documented; and second, as an equally elaborate material and building technique, of which virtually nothing is said. It is as if there were not one, but two people at work in JP (or perhaps two works to consider at once): an applied mathematician who sees the work as *process* and wants to clarify everything; and an artist who sees the work as *product* and will dissemble his motives behind an aesthetic fact. The two personas do not coordinate that well

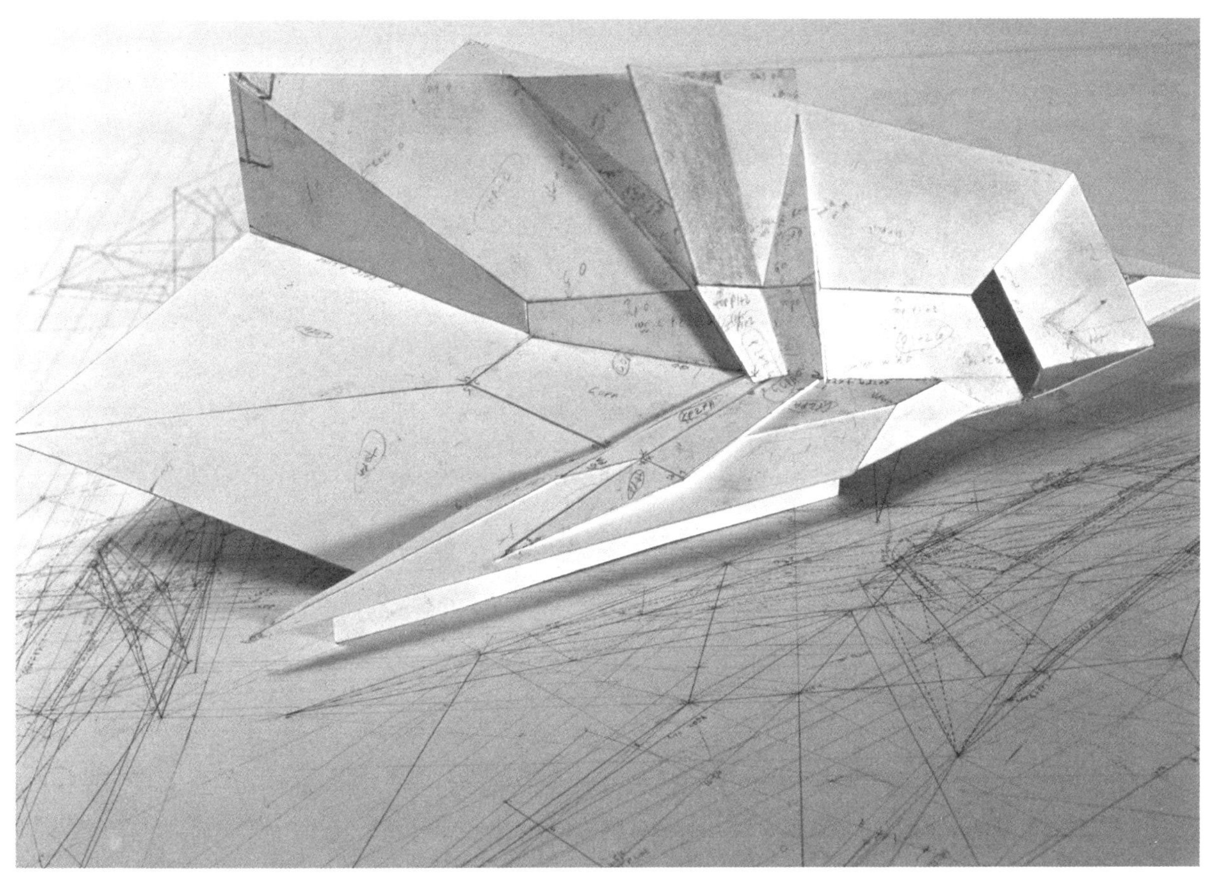

Preston Scott Cohen,
Stereotomic permutations:
patterns for head-start facilities,
1994. Courtesy of the architect.

because neither needs the other to fulfil itself. If the work were
pure process, the final model would have to be different:
JP would use some rapid prototyping or laser-cutting technology
whose primary function is not to automate a task (a trivial and
incidental benefit) *but to seamlessly translate the abstraction of
the mathematical process into matter.* Such a model would be free
of what Chris Wise terms 'imperfections' – and, by the same
token, artistically worthless. If, on the other hand, JP's work were
pure product, he would have to admit that no amount of inversion can explain, justify, let alone legitimise the delicate trans-
lucencies of the *Klein bottle* and *Cross-cap* sculptures, the coarse
vigour of the timber in *Spiral motion*, or the milky depth of the
plaster spheres. These breathtaking pieces rely primarily on
material effect. The material effect is paramount, but compared
to the abstraction of the mathematical original, it is also *excessive:* if JP's work were pure process, the expressiveness of the
material effect would be redundant and unwelcome. Personally
I much prefer to read JP's sculpture as an actual work of art,
where 'imperfection' reigns supreme and the mathematical
demonstration plays second fiddle to sheer aesthetic presence,
provided that the mathematician in JP allows me to bypass his
original intentions.

JP's way is figurative, rather than abstract. However unlikely
a critique to level at something so explicitly mathematical, the
statement holds. Consider the following fact: when the photographs of JP's sculptures are reduced and reproduced in contact
sheet form, the sculptures *look like buildings* (of a rather monu-
mental kind); when reproduced in a larger format, they do not
look like anything in particular. Is this misperception only a fac-
tor of distance? The reason is the following: the proportions of
many of JP's sculptures are similar to those of buildings; and the
sculptures always sit on a base. Chris Wise has noted, rightly,
that JP will only use a handful of the available points obtained
by inversion. That is a common dilemma for those who manipu-
late equations in visual terms: how dense should the *range* of an
equation be? Or, put in other terms, how many points does one
need in order to plot a curve? Given the overall dimensions of
the model (its width and length) and the thickness of the card
used to cut the profiles, JP's choice of a range is such that the
proportion of the gap between stacked profiles is rather like
that of a full building floor; it is my private conjecture that JP
sees them as floors to begin with. Then there are the bases.
Since the transformation of figures by inversion unfolds in space
and the properties of the inverted figures are equivalent in all
three dimensions, there is no need, mathematically speaking,

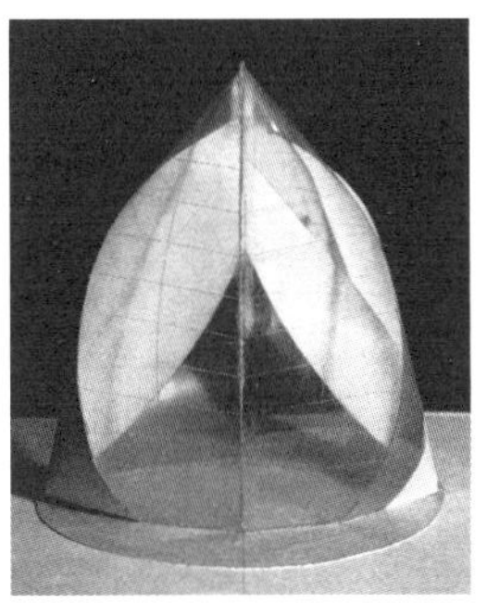
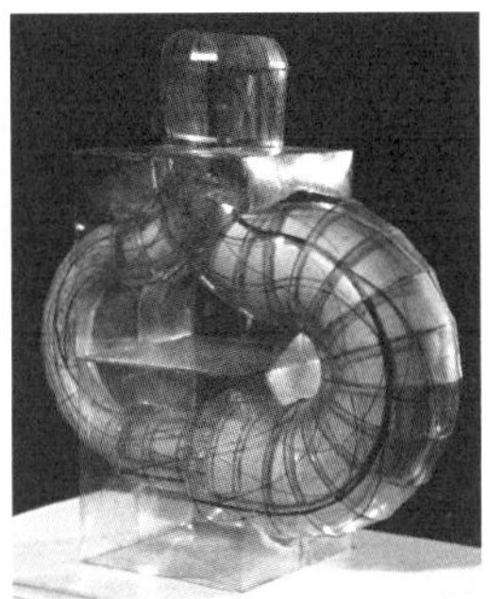
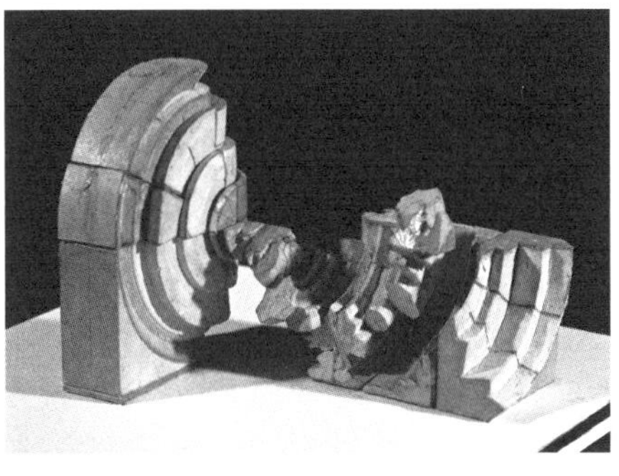

Above from left to right:
Cross-cap, Klein bottle and
Spiral motion sculptures. Also
shown on pp. 41 and 48-49.

for a base. Is its presence a concession to the demands of fabrication? In most cases it does appear to be holding the sculpture together, but that is only by choice: as physical manifestations of a continuous mathematical relation, the material bits of JP's sculpture are always connected – it would have been fairly simple to turn them into a self-supporting assemblage. Stability is not the problem. The base is there for an altogether different reason. It indicates that there is a *preferred orientation* to the inverted surface, made manifest by the presence of a *ground plane*. The presence of this ground plane compounds the effect of the sculpture's chosen proportions in a very specific manner: together they remove a great deal of abstraction from the sculpt ure and turn it into a *figurative* object, easily misread as a building. Figuration is not a problem per se; it is just that it runs counter to what projective geometry is rather good at: the ability to establish and reflect on abstract relations between forms without the conveyance of their iconic status (what the forms 'look like' or 'remind us of'). In those terms the descent into figuration is also a loss of information.

Incidentally, at JP's request, his early life-drawings of bodies were on display alongside his later abstract sculpture at the major retrospective of his work held at the Architectural Association in 2002. In hindsight the juxtaposition makes a lot of sense: as the drawings attest, JP was a figurative artist; likewise he is a figurative mathematician. And hence, under certain conditions, his abstract sculptures look like buildings to us; which is why they are critically praised by a number of seasoned architecture professionals who usually have less time for similar experiments conducted exclusively in abstract mode (the Young Turks who

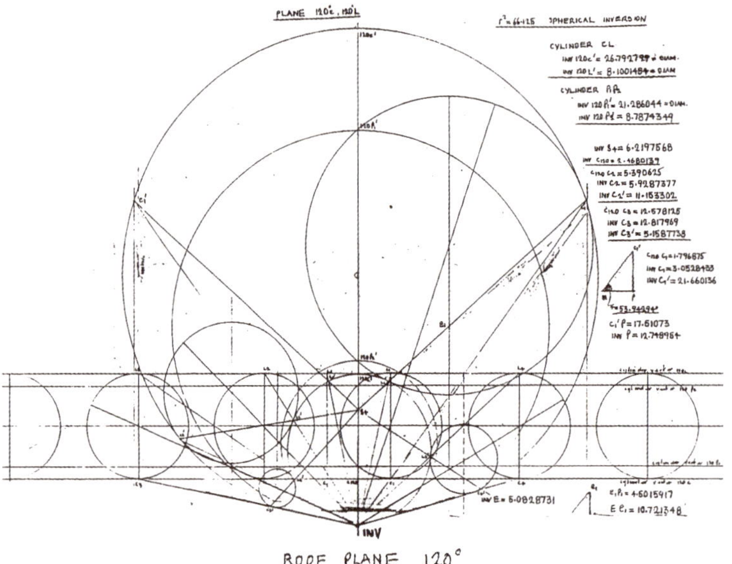

A geometric progression of spheres inverted with respect to a point not lying on the surface of any sphere or the three cones' 30°, 40°, 50° vertical axis. Roof plane. See pp. 28-29 for main plane and pp. 60-61 for model view.

explore the speculative side of architecture through geometry today have long given up on figuration).

JP's way is compositional, rather than transformation-based. This assertion is both true and false. His work is unquestionably transformation-based: he produces his sculpture through the rigorous application of the principle of inversion. Eventually the value of rigour is debatable. As Chris Wise points out, transformations are applied wholesale to figures: there is no room for adjusting the results or tweaking the process on an ad hoc basis; to be rigorous is also to be constrained. And yet, several of JP's sculptures exhibit the sort of delightful *piecemeal quality* that does not quite evoke the brute force of wholesale conversion. *Inversion from cylinder with ball*, in particular, is made of several pieces of various forms and sizes (planar, cylindrical, spherical); some pieces are tangent to others; some are solid; the variations in scale can be significant; and the use of distinct materials (plaster of Paris, card, steel rods) reinforces their individuality. Clearly JP positions the operands of the inversion so as to produce a carefully calibrated piecemeal result, which in architectural parlance looks and feels extremely *composed*. Thus JP's work presents us with a conundrum: *it is both compositional and transformation-based.* For all its elemental rigidity (every part of the sculpture remains a clearly legible geometric figure), it exhibits the conceptual flexibility of an architectural composition in which spatial effects are deployed to measure. In this narrow sense JP's sculpture is truly architectural, but there

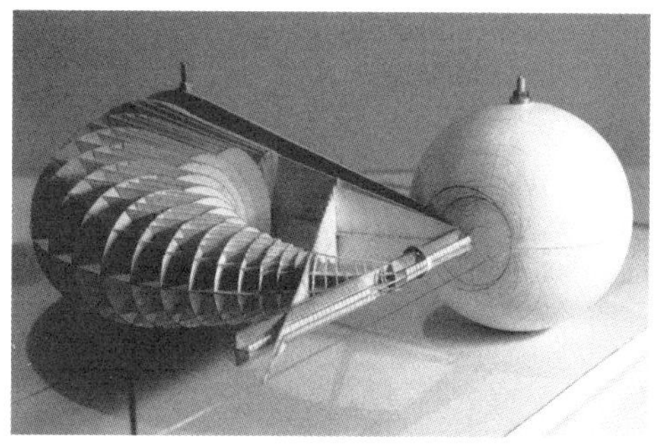
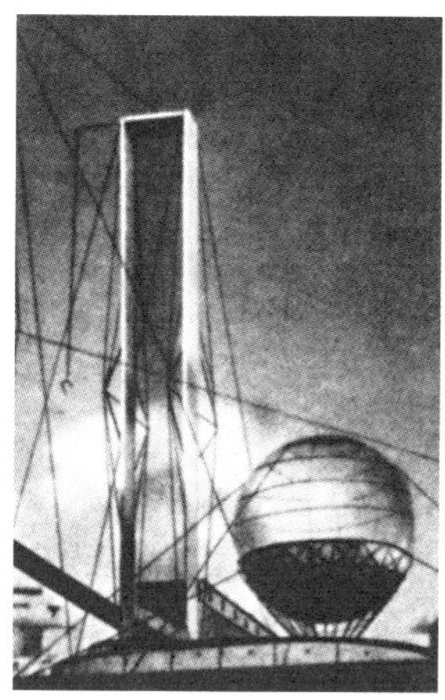

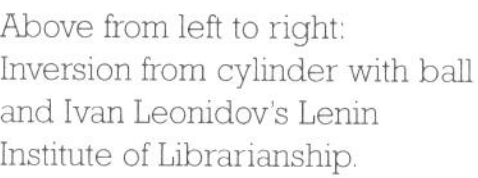
Above from left to right:
Inversion from cylinder with ball
and Ivan Leonidov's Lenin
Institute of Librarianship.

are pros and cons to the affiliation: the status of architectural composition is presently at an all-time low, and that can only harm the truly critical reception of JP's work. With its elegant juxtapositions of geometric figures (plane, cylinder, sphere), it is more likely to remind us of the unbuilt architectural proposals inspired by suprematist painting in the 1920s, than of anything contemporary. *Inversion from cylinder with ball* has a lot more in common with, say, Ivan Leonidov's wondrous Lenin Institute of Librarianship (1927) than with any equivalent proposal emanating from today's architectural avant-garde, in which the use of geometry would be invariably polemic – and figuration and composition strictly banned.[i]

JP's way is slow and manual, rather than fast and mechanised. That seems to be a defining characteristic of his art. But JP's relationship to the computer and its meta-mechanical functions (or the lack thereof) is also enigmatic. As I argued earlier after examining the respective merits of process versus product in his work, JP's endeavours are split into two competing halves by his avoidance (no doubt out of necessity) of digital fabrication machinery. Bringing them back together with the help of the computer would require sacrificing the sophisticated material craft, which, in my opinion at least, is the more intriguing half. I do not have a problem with JP's rejection of the medium of computation. He may not use it, but his strategy of pre-rationalising spatial figures is inherently computational, in spirit anyway. While he does not have access to software himself, his instru-

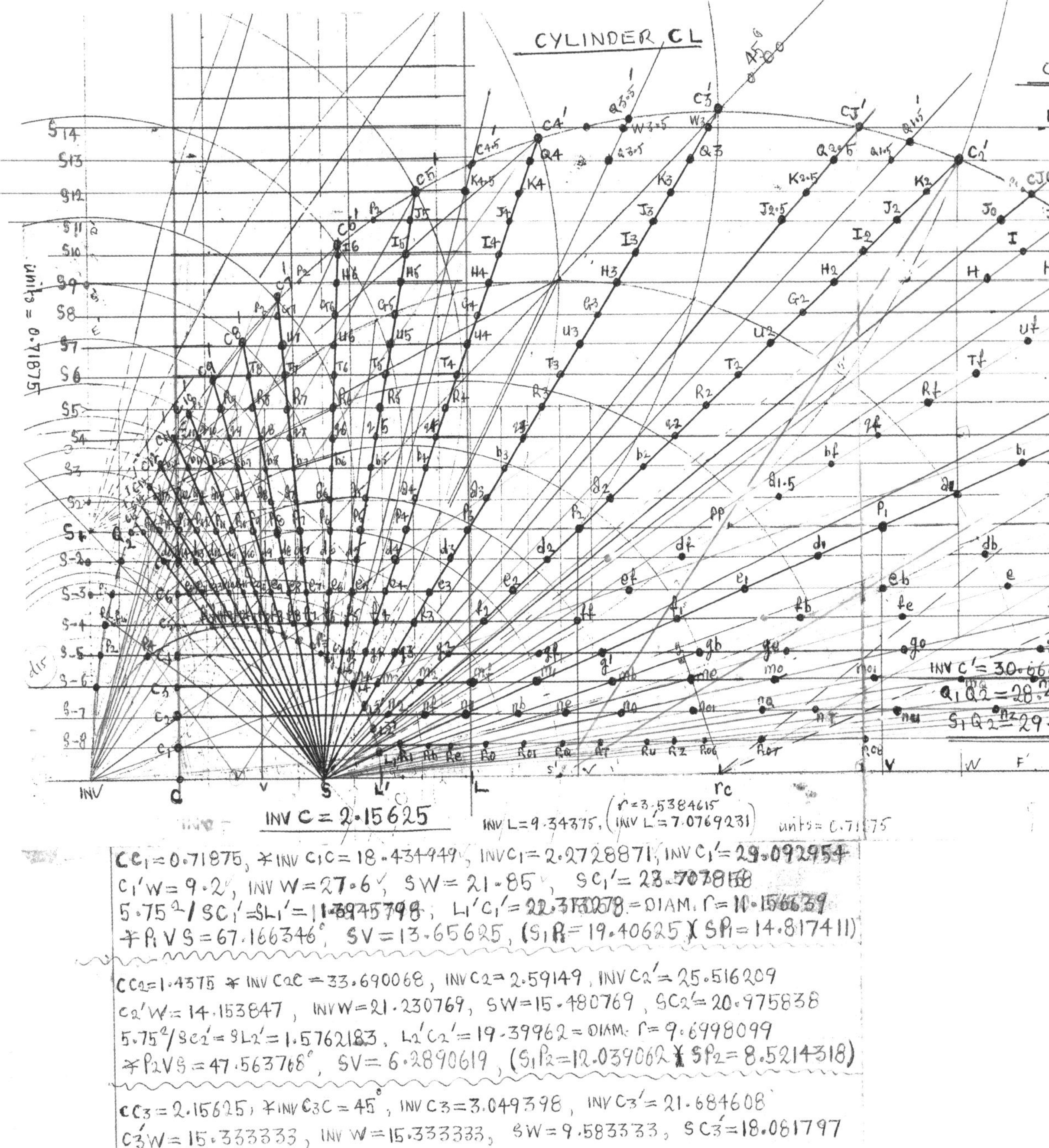

Inverting a cylinder CL with respect to a point not lying on the cylinder. The resulting cylinder is subject to reflection and rotation, therefore three cyclides intersect one another. See pp. 36-37 for model view.

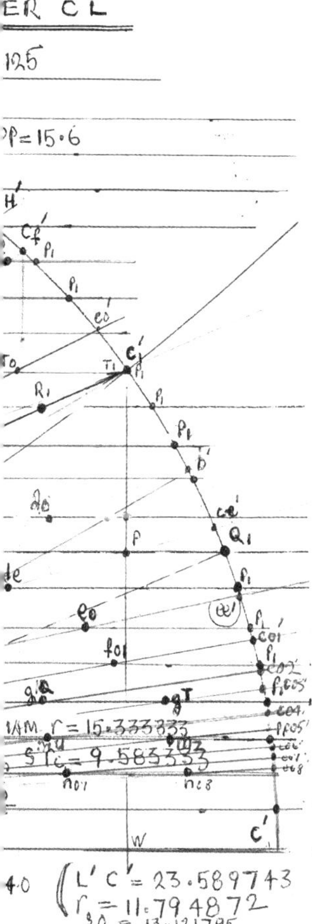

mental outlook resembles, often enough, that of a software designer (minus the loops, obviously, since he does not acknowledge the need for iteration). This is already more than most technologically savvy architects can claim.

JP's singular process has more unexpected implications in store. No doubt the object of a personal secret, his 'slowness' is telling nonetheless. For one thing it confirms what everyone who has invested a lot of energy in computer-aided design must have experienced first hand: how slow, how painfully labour-intensive the design and fabrication of a pliant surface can be! During the decade-and-a-half that saw modelling software replace the drawing board, and fabrication machinery become commonplace, the time spent working out the odds and ends of pliant form has not decreased – it has increased. This is not only due to an absolute increase of workload. The task of rationalising a three-dimensional surface at the scale of an architectural proposal (and building so much as a simple mockup) is not only complicated, it is often so repetitious that even modelling software may no longer be of substantial help, and scripting or computer programming must be brought on board to consolidate the numerous batches of meta-mechanical tasks. Beginning from the surface's generative lines, the man-hours required to produce an adequate, laser cutter-compliant cutting template (and the boredom attendant to it) are not essentially dissimilar to those consumed in cutting card by hand. Since JP's work does not predate the widespread use of computer-aided design and fabrication, it would be far-fetched to call him a precursor, although his slow art, in which pace plays such a vital part, clarifies an essential aspect of our own computerised practices. Like a mime performance in which all notions are pared down to a minimum, and the richness of human gesture is decanted into a single nod, JP's way reveals something otherwise invisible which had been there all along, warning us of the grim sterilities of meta-mechanical repetition, and showing us exactly how to get there.

George L. Legendre

1   The affinity with I. Leonidov's work is one of material too. Leonidov made wonderful models whose grip on the imagination remains greater than that of his drawings.

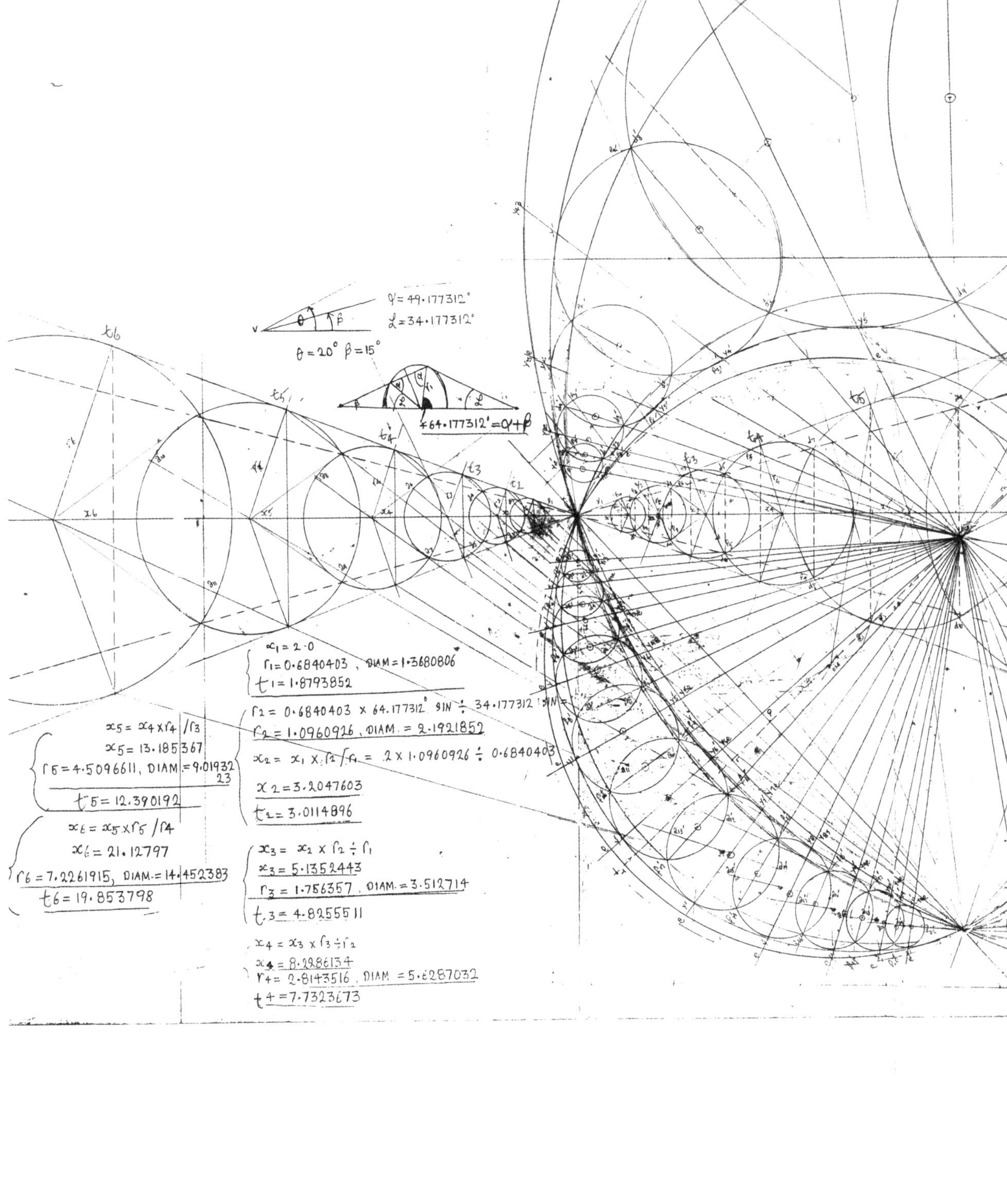

γ = 49·177312°
∠ = 34·177312°
θ = 20° β = 15°
∠64·177312' = α+β

x₅ = x₄ × r₄ / r₃
x₅ = 13·185367
r₅ = 4·5096611, DIAM = 9·01932 23
t₅ = 12·390192

x₆ = x₅ × r₅ / r₄
x₆ = 21·12797
r₆ = 7·2261915, DIAM = 14·452383
t₆ = 19·853798

α₁ = 2·0
r₁ = 0·6840403, DIAM = 1·3680806
t₁ = 1·8793852

r₂ = 0·6840403 × 64·177312° SIN ÷ 34·177312° SIN =
r₂ = 1·0960926, DIAM = 2·1921852
x₂ = x₁ × r₂/r₁ = 2 × 1·0960926 ÷ 0·6840403
x₂ = 3·2047603
t₂ = 3·0114896

x₃ = x₂ × r₂ ÷ r₁
x₃ = 5·1352443
r₃ = 1·756357, DIAM = 3·512714
t₃ = 4·8255511

x₄ = x₃ × r₃ ÷ r₂
x₄ = 8·2286134
r₄ = 2·8143516, DIAM = 5·6287032
t₄ = 7·7323673

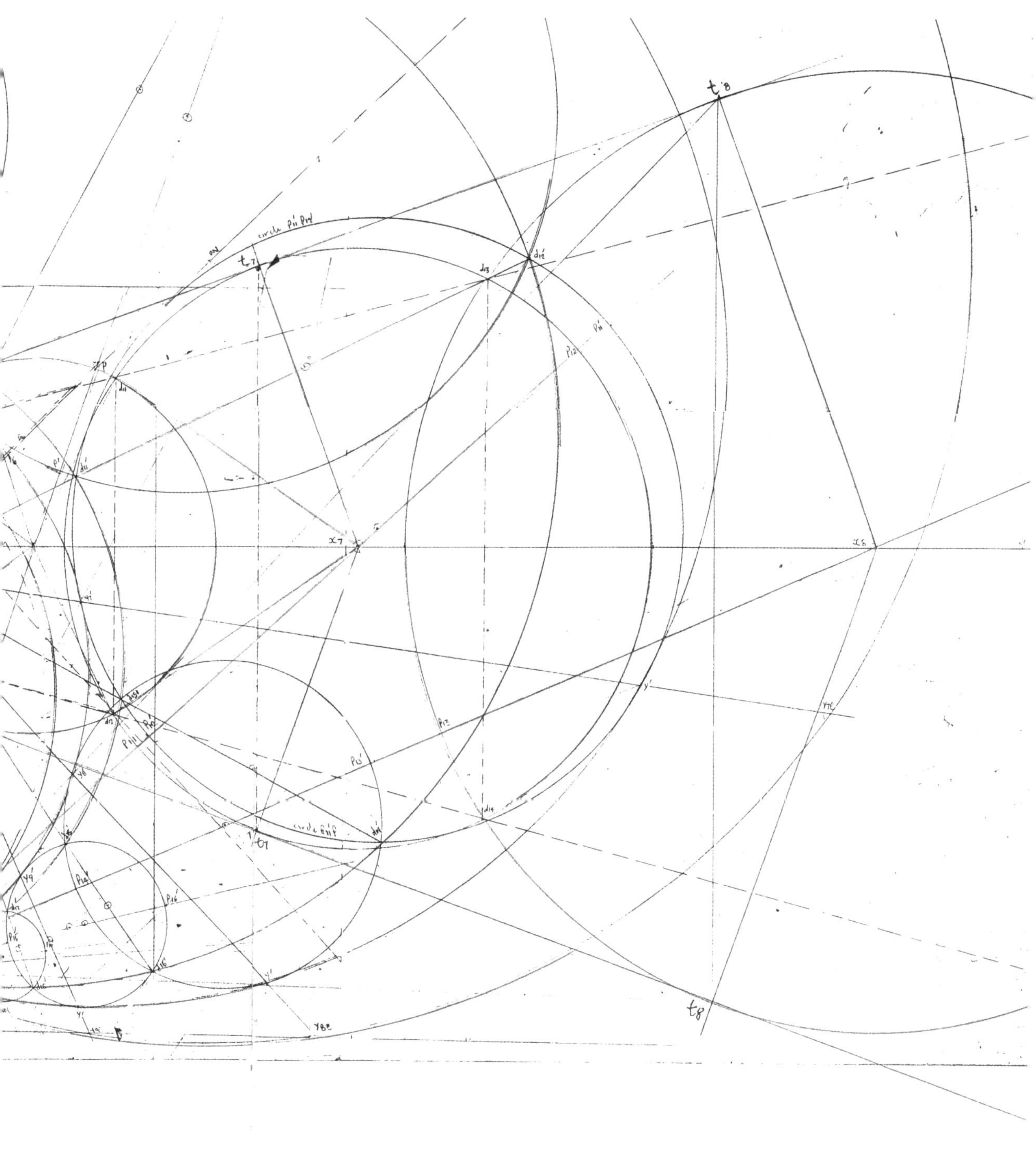

Spherical inversion. Inverting intersecting spheres whose centres lie on the axis of a cylinder, with respect to a point not lying on any of the spheres. See pp. 60-61 for model view.

Music and the inversion principle

The inversion principle can be used for transforming one thing into another, for both large- and small-scale form. It produces a certain skeletal consistency but is not the rigid system one might suppose, as it allows the artist imaginative choices and flexibility, enabling personality to be imposed as part of the process. Logic is nothing to be afraid of when applied to art; it is simply part of human thought, spatial relations, balance and the law of nature. It is the human imprint on the method of inversion that is of real significance.

The relation between the inversion principle and music is one of similarity rather than exactitude. The twelve-note method, as devised by Arnold Schoenberg, is in essence a simple device for ensuring complete structural unity in the spheres of melody and harmony. It affirms the unity of musical space and the relationship of all ideas in a work.

The twelve-note series takes four equally important forms: the original, the original inverted (so that each interval falls instead of rising and vice versa), the retrograde (the original series played in reverse), and the retrograde of the inversion. This is analogous to the points A and B inside the circle of inversion and the points B' and A' outside the circle of inversion.

Using the sphere of inversion, when the infinite number of points surrounding the sphere are inverted to inside the sphere,

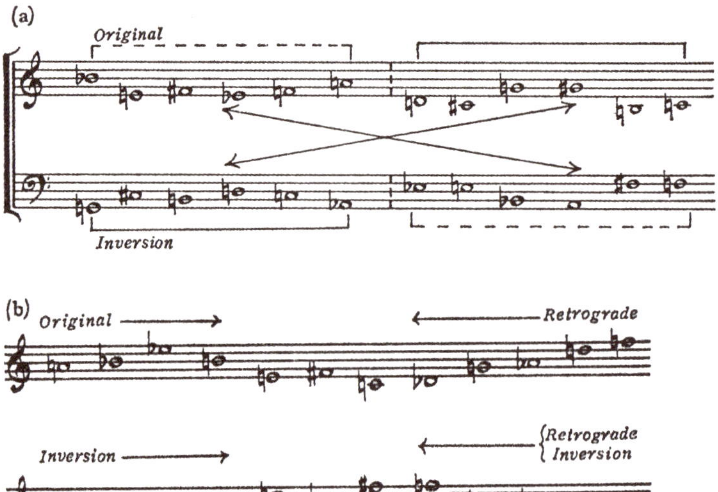

The four forms of Schoenberg's twelve-note melodies.

the points become more compact the nearer they are to the centre of the sphere (the centre of inversion). If these points are interpreted as sound, then a stage is reached when one musical note cannot be distinguished from another and the sound becomes an intense and dense noise. This feeling of angst seems to flow through most of the music of the Second Viennese School, as reflected in the works of Schoenberg, Berg and Webern. The same effect can be achieved with $MP \cdot MQ = MR^2$.

Karlheinz Stockhausen has forged a new musical language that has profoundly inspired me, giving rise to various parallels in my work. For example, in his *Kontakte*, the composer uses what he calls 'moment form' to make 'vertical incisions' that 'break through the horizontal concept of time'. In *Klavierstück X*, he includes long silences when the listener is meant to complete the space from his memory of what has gone before.

Stockhausen has thus introduced a completely revolutionary way of listening to music, and I see this music as enfolded within the beauty of the sensual spatial curves of inversion. I like to imagine Stockhausen's music being performed inside one of my own structures (made on a grand scale), so that the sensuality of the music emanates from the curvaceous sculpture around it.

Fractals is an area of mathematics that I am now moving towards. Intuitively, I feel it may provide me with a further insight into the nature of Stockhausen's composition.

John Pickering

WORKS

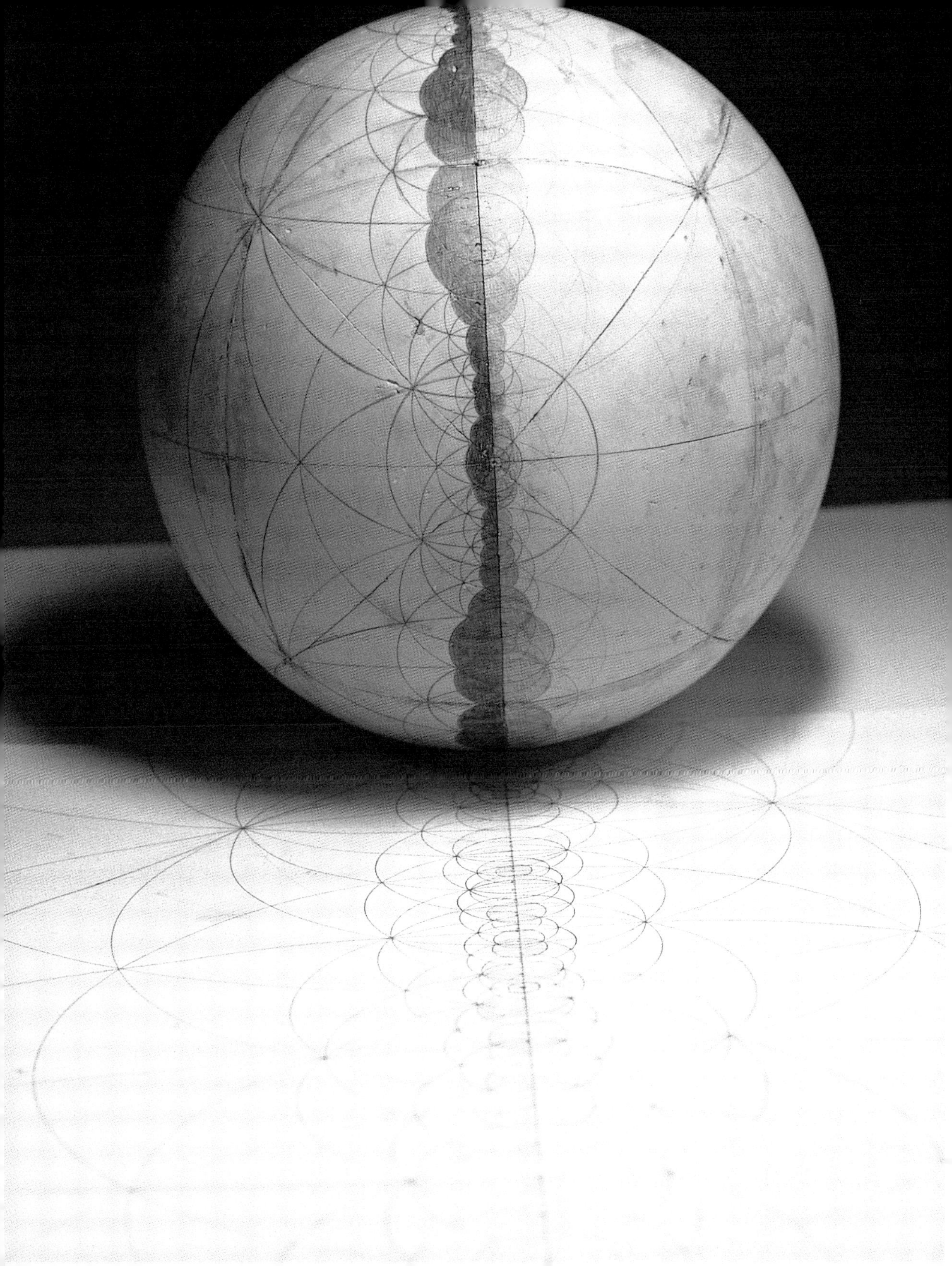

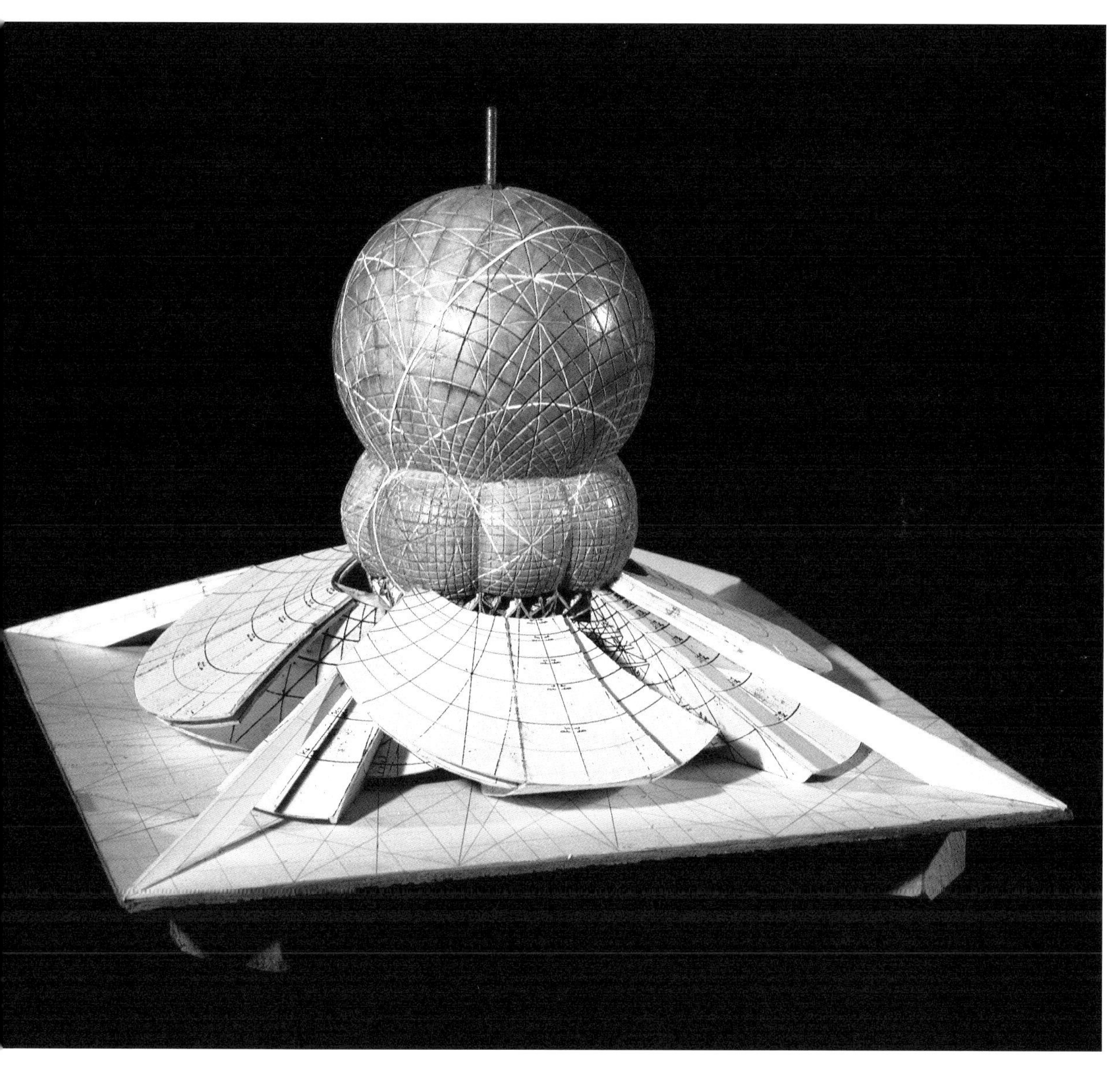

Inverting a three-dimensional square grid
where the centre of inversion lies inside
the grid, 1981–1983–1984.
Plaster of Paris, card, wood and steel rod,
32.5 cm x 32.5 cm x 20 cm.

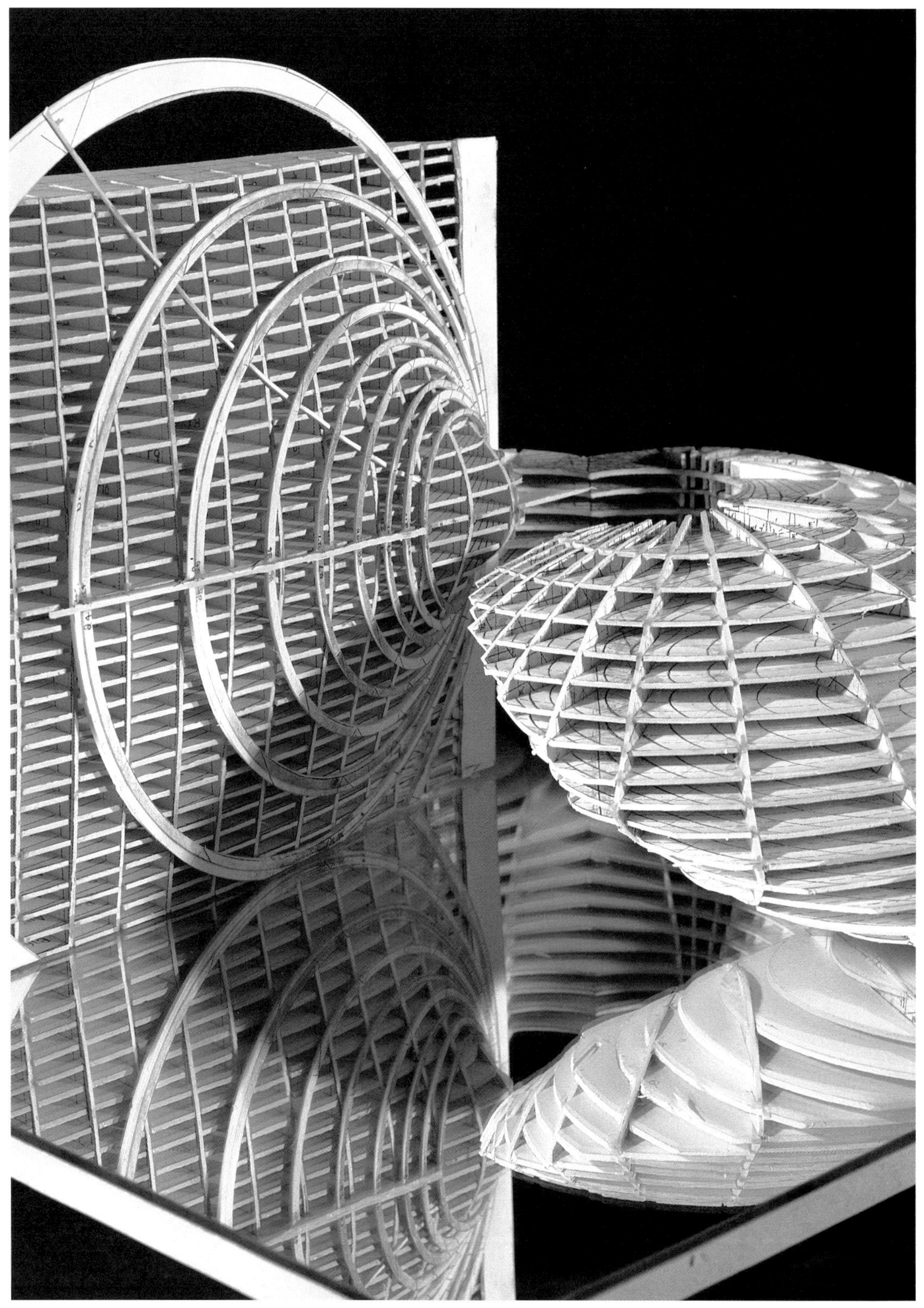

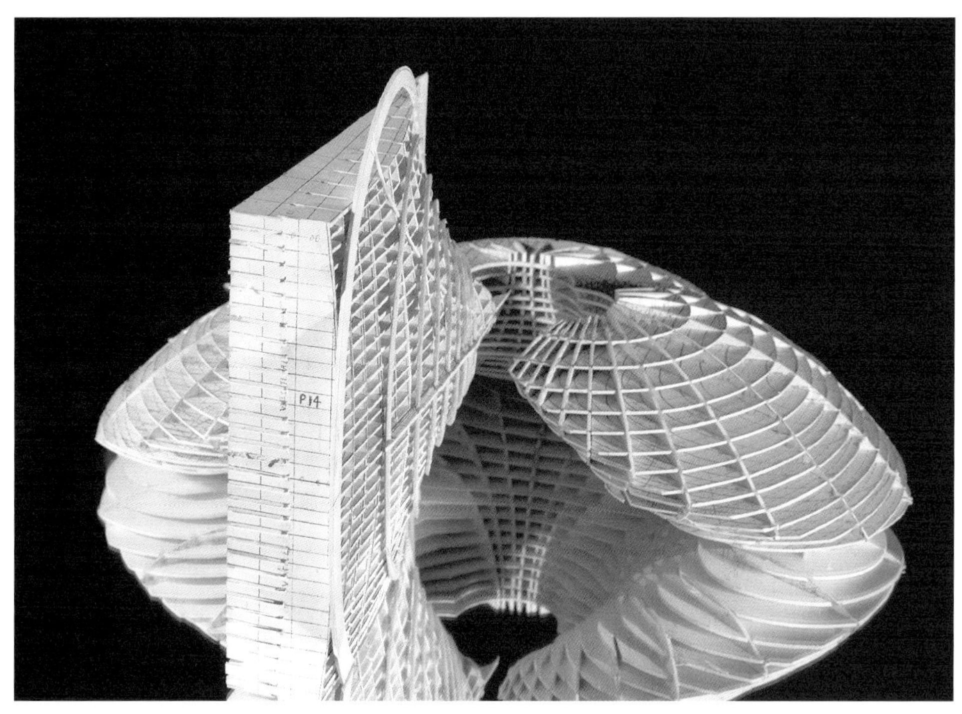

Inverting a cylinder CL with respect to a point not lying on the cylinder. The resulting cyclide is then subjected to reflection and rotation, therefore three cyclides intersect one another. Inverting a second cylinder with respect to a point lying on the cylinder, the resulting cyclide takes up the fourth position, November 1998–January 2002.
Card, glass, mirror, 62 cm x 57 cm x 28 cm.

Inverting a cylinder AB where the centre of inversion does not lie on the
cylinder. Parallel horizontal planes have been inverted back onto the cylinder;
these are wraparound ellipses. The 'helicopter platform' intersecting the
cylinder is an upside-down geodesic dome, September 1990–April 1992.
Card, cardboard cylinder, steel rods, 63 cm x 88 cm x 20 cm.

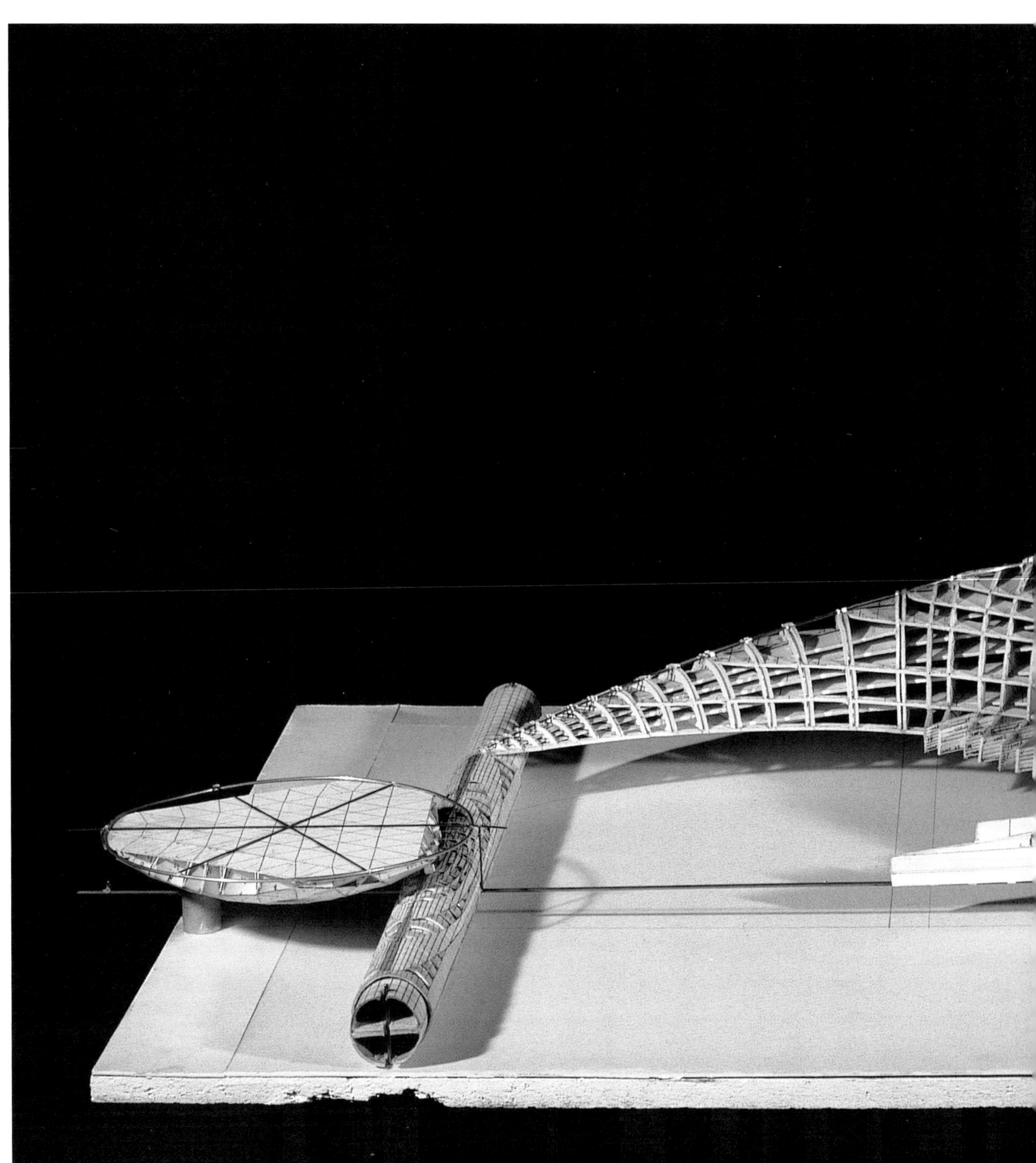

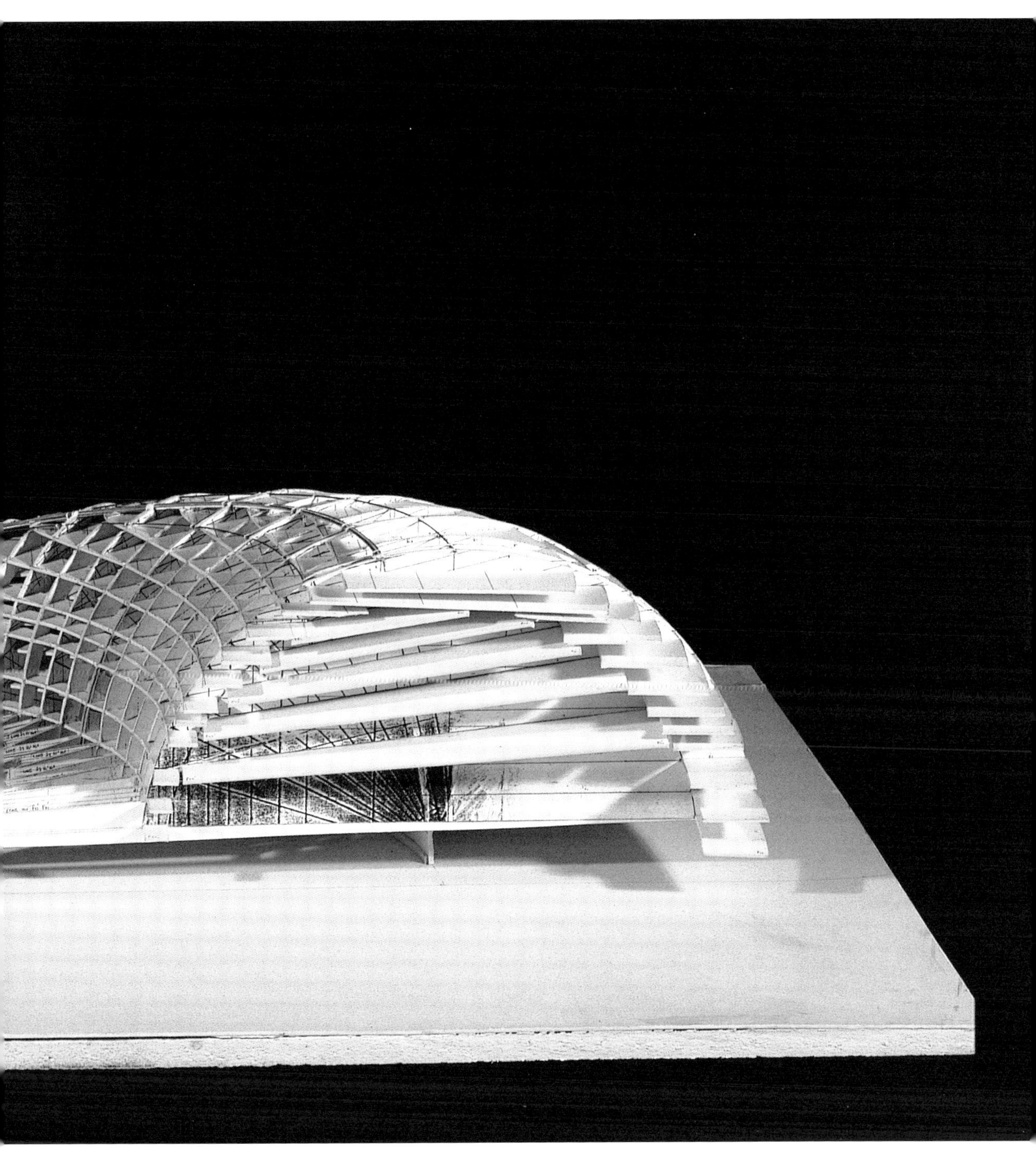

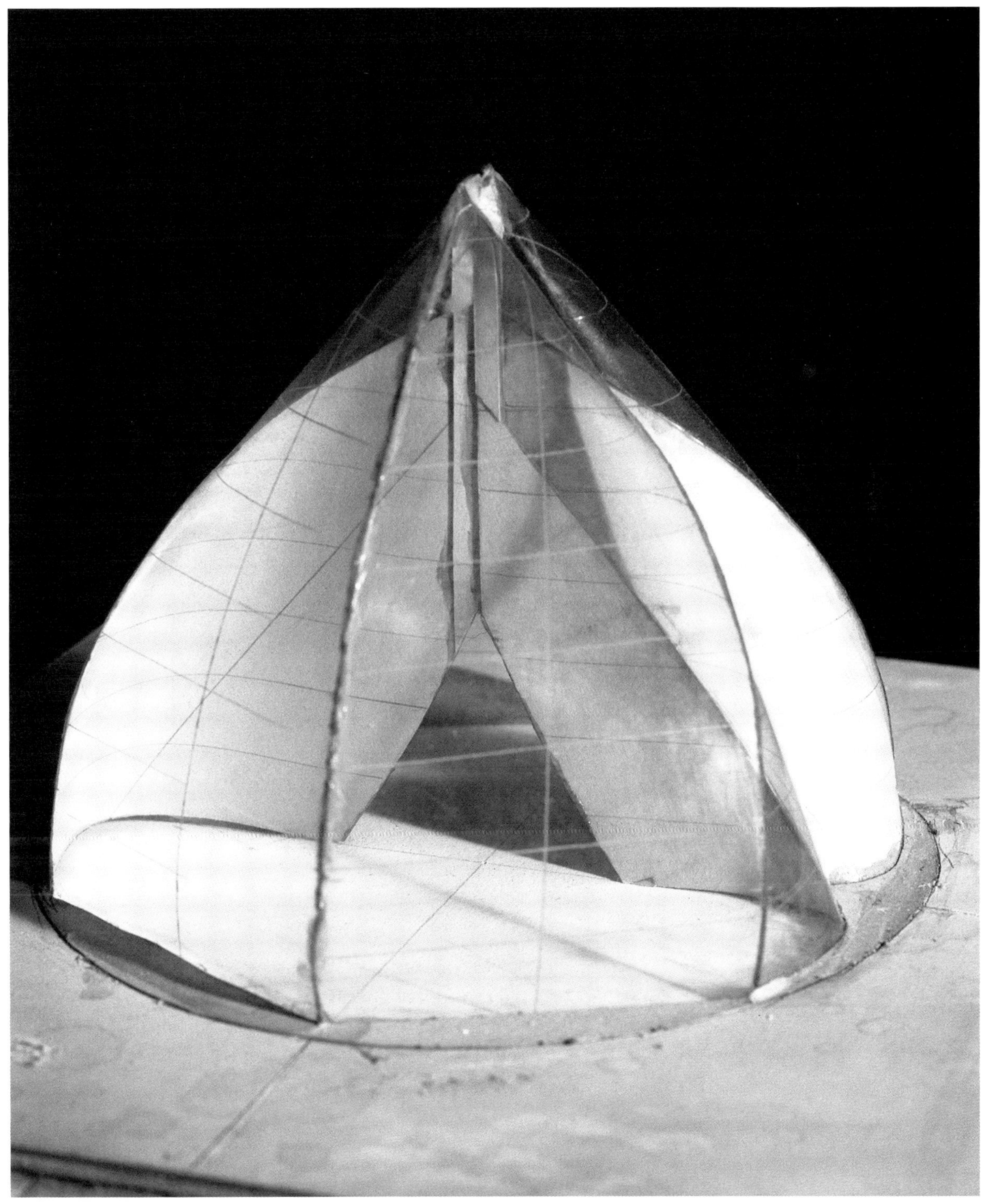

Cross-cap, a one-sided surface, 1973.
Acetate and card, 12 cm x 14 cm x 14 cm.

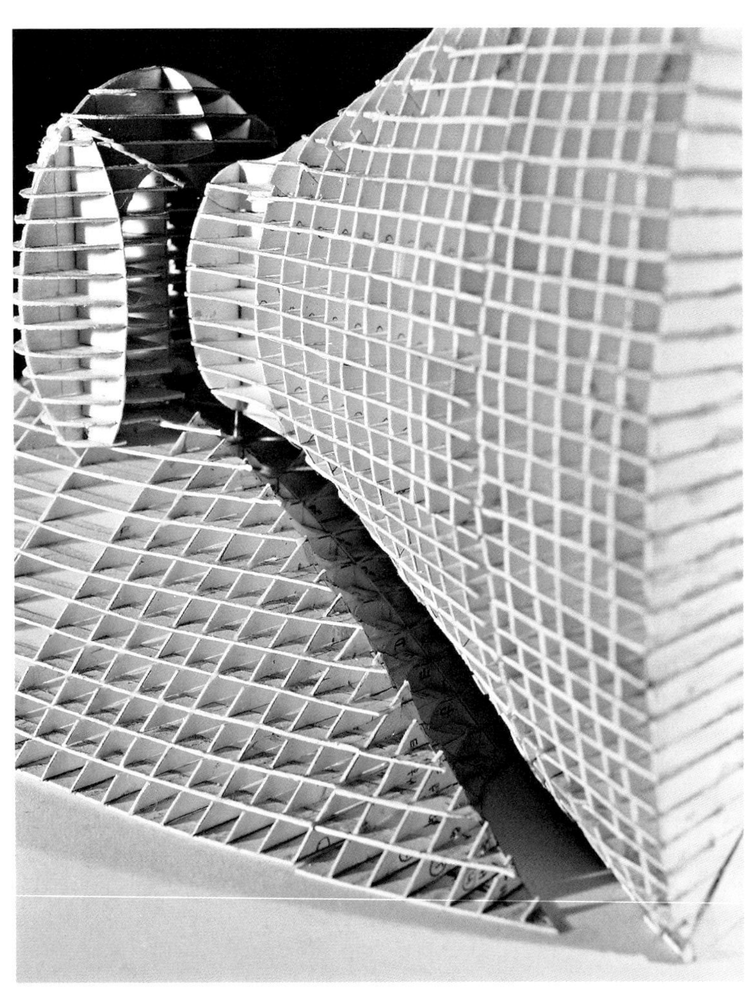

Ellipsoid, one half of the hyperboloid of
two sheets, one half of the hyperboloid
of one sheet, 1971–1972–1973.
Card, 14 cm x 27 cm x 19 cm.

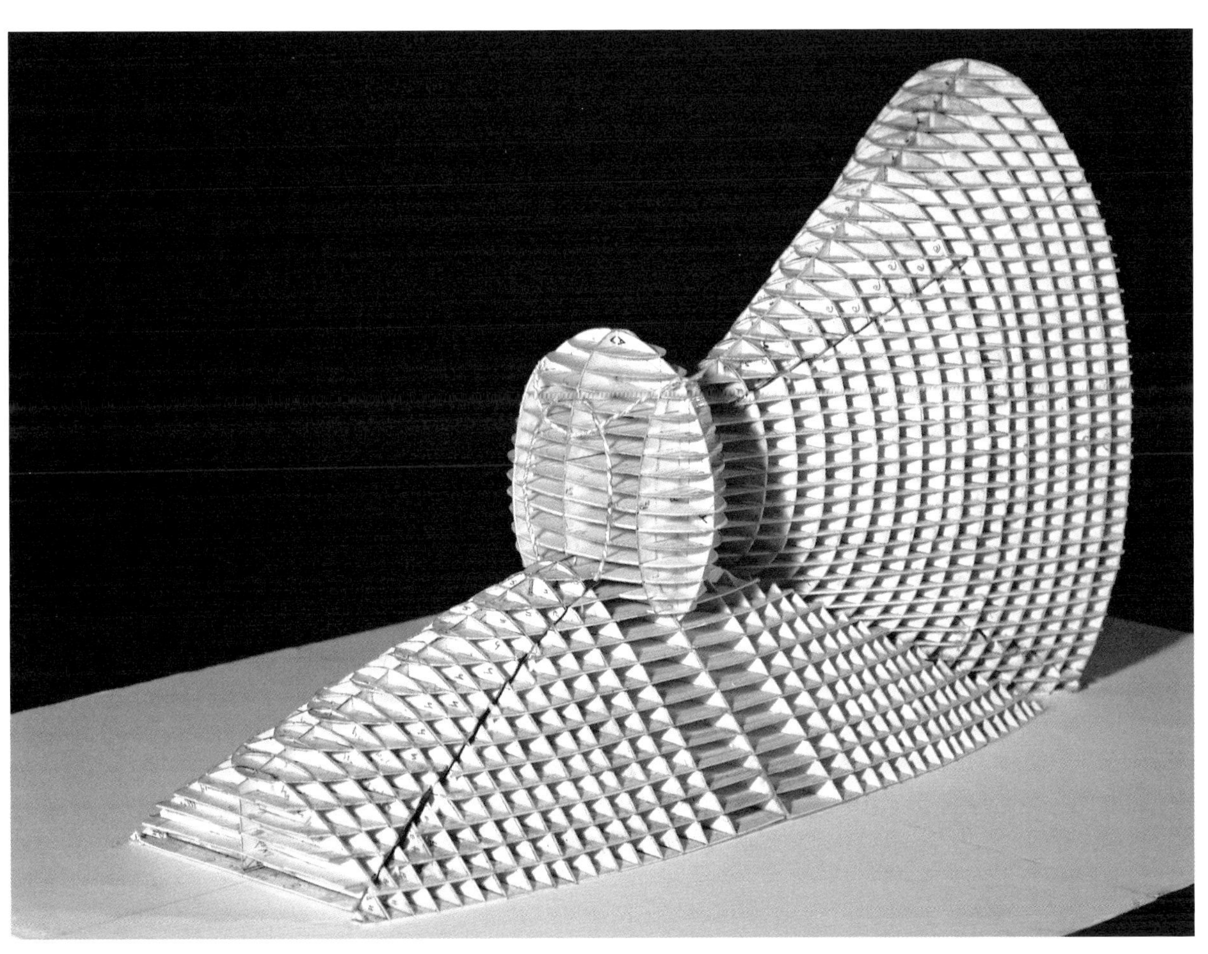

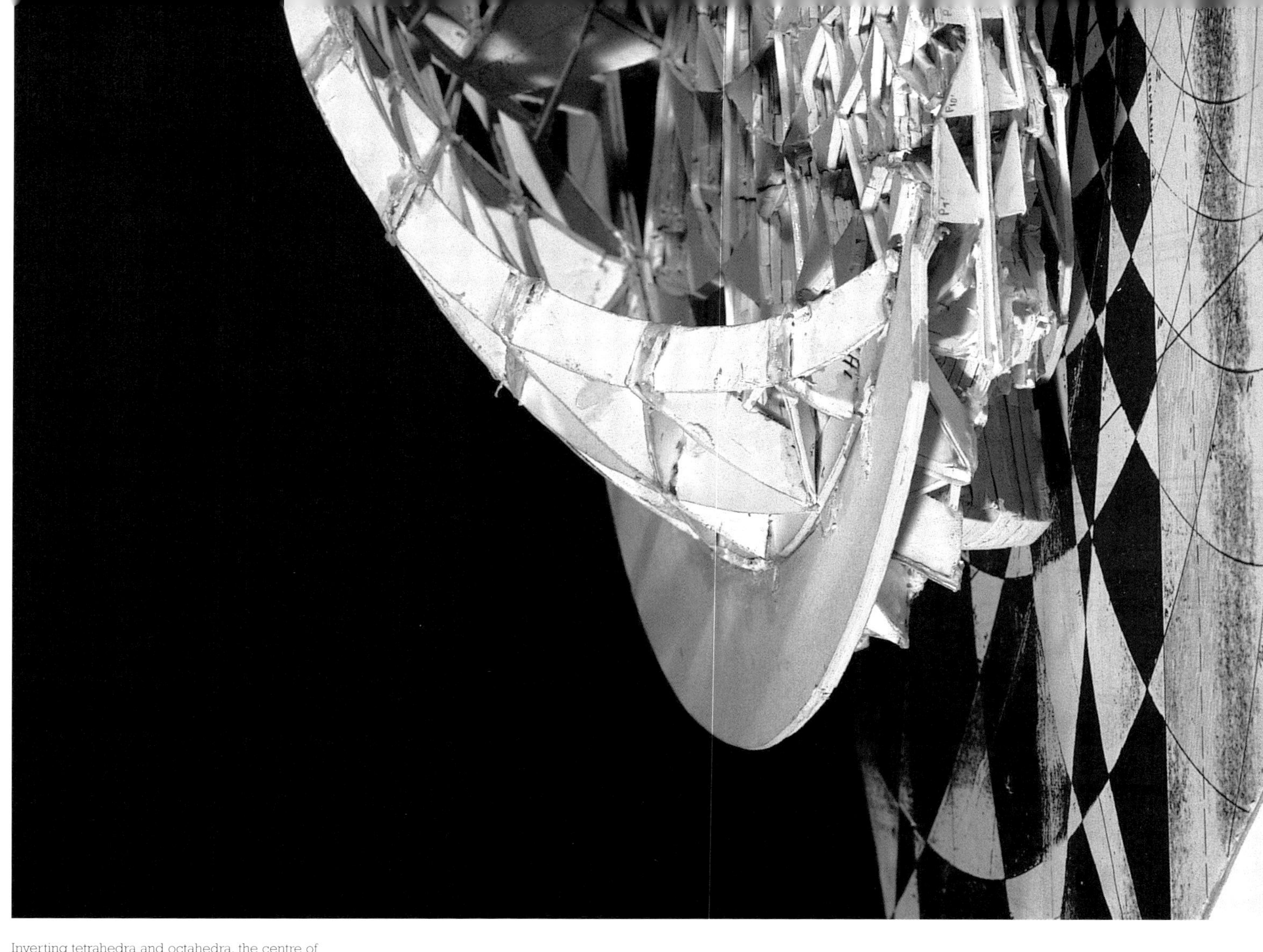

Inverting tetrahedra and octahedra, the centre of
inversion lying off the tetrahedra and octahedra,
March 1996–September 1998.
Card, wire mesh, plaster of Paris,
80 cm x 60 cm x 26 cm.

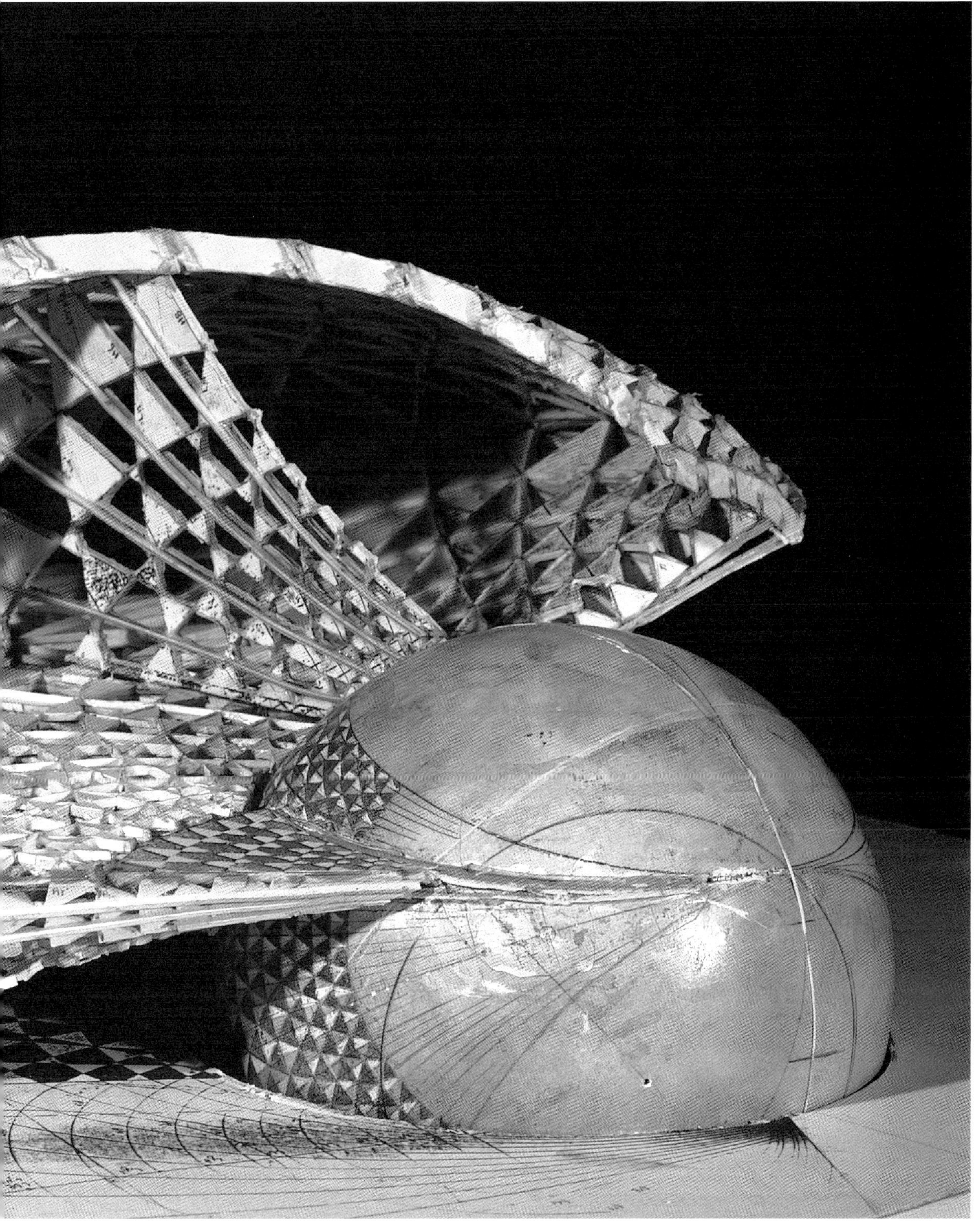

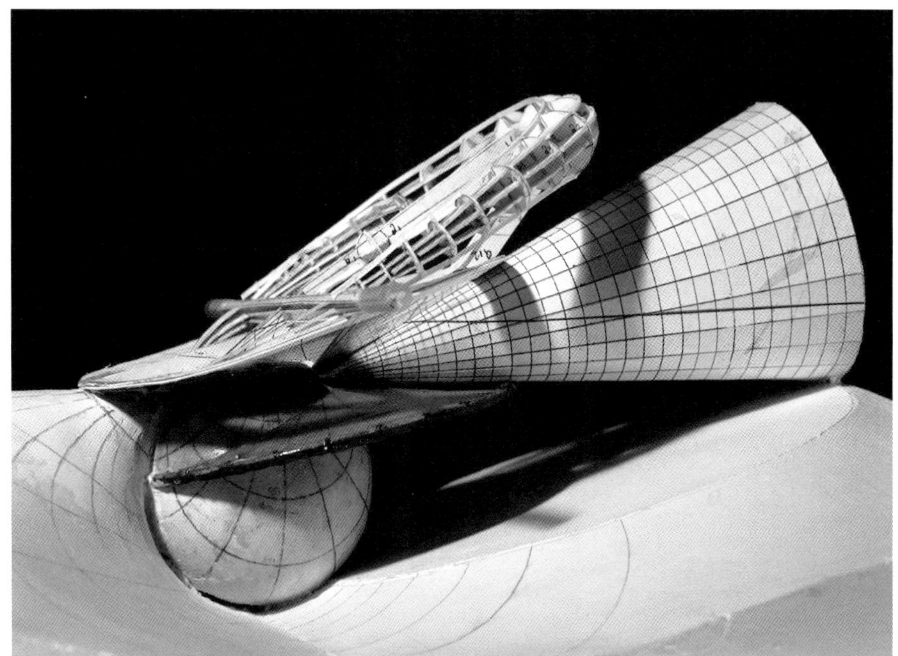

Inverting two circular cones, the centre of inversion lying on
the two cones, and inverting a cylinder, the centre of inversion not lying on the cylinder, August 1987–April 1988.
Plaster of Paris, card and steel rods, 35 cm x 29 cm x 14 cm.

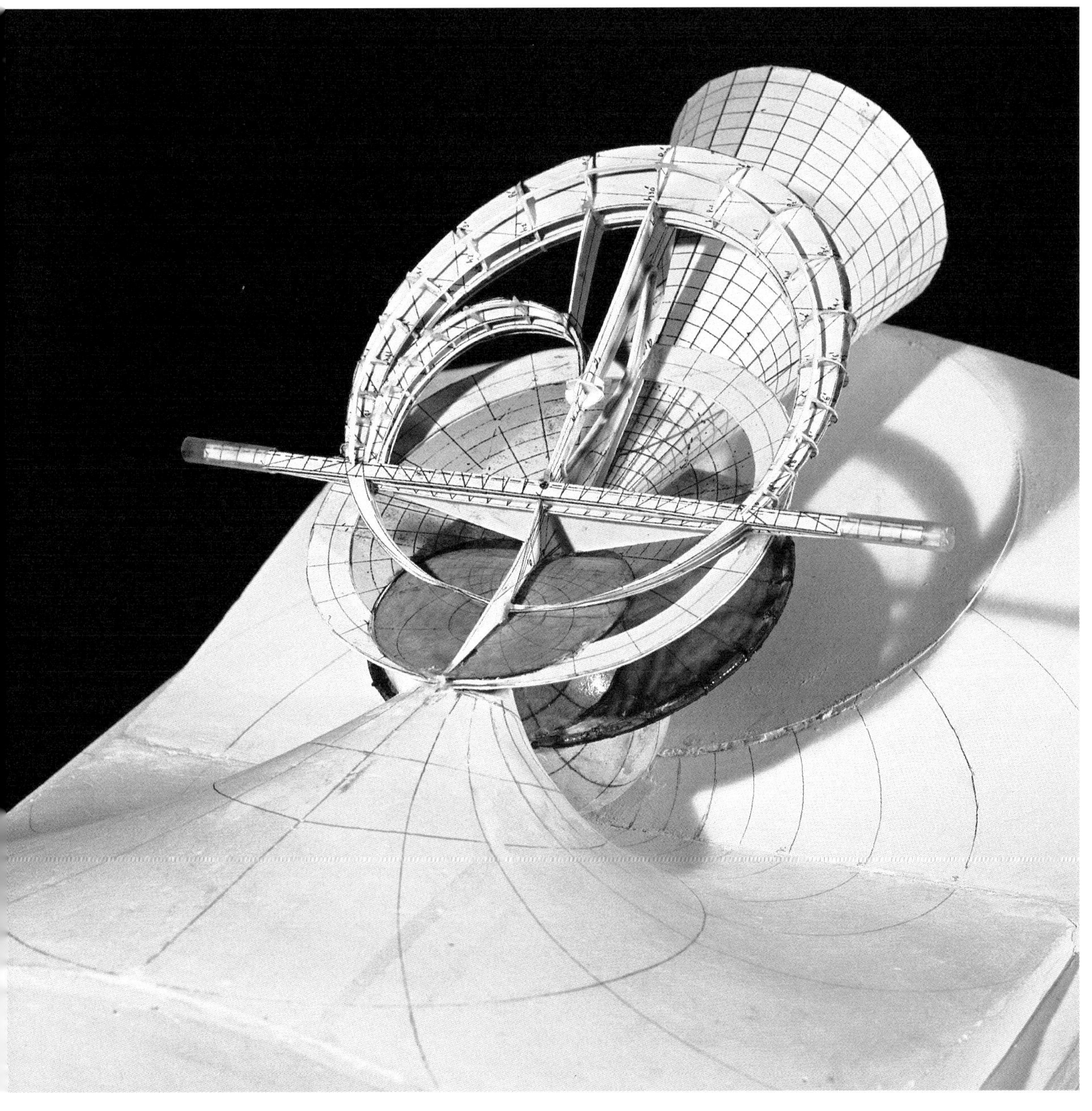

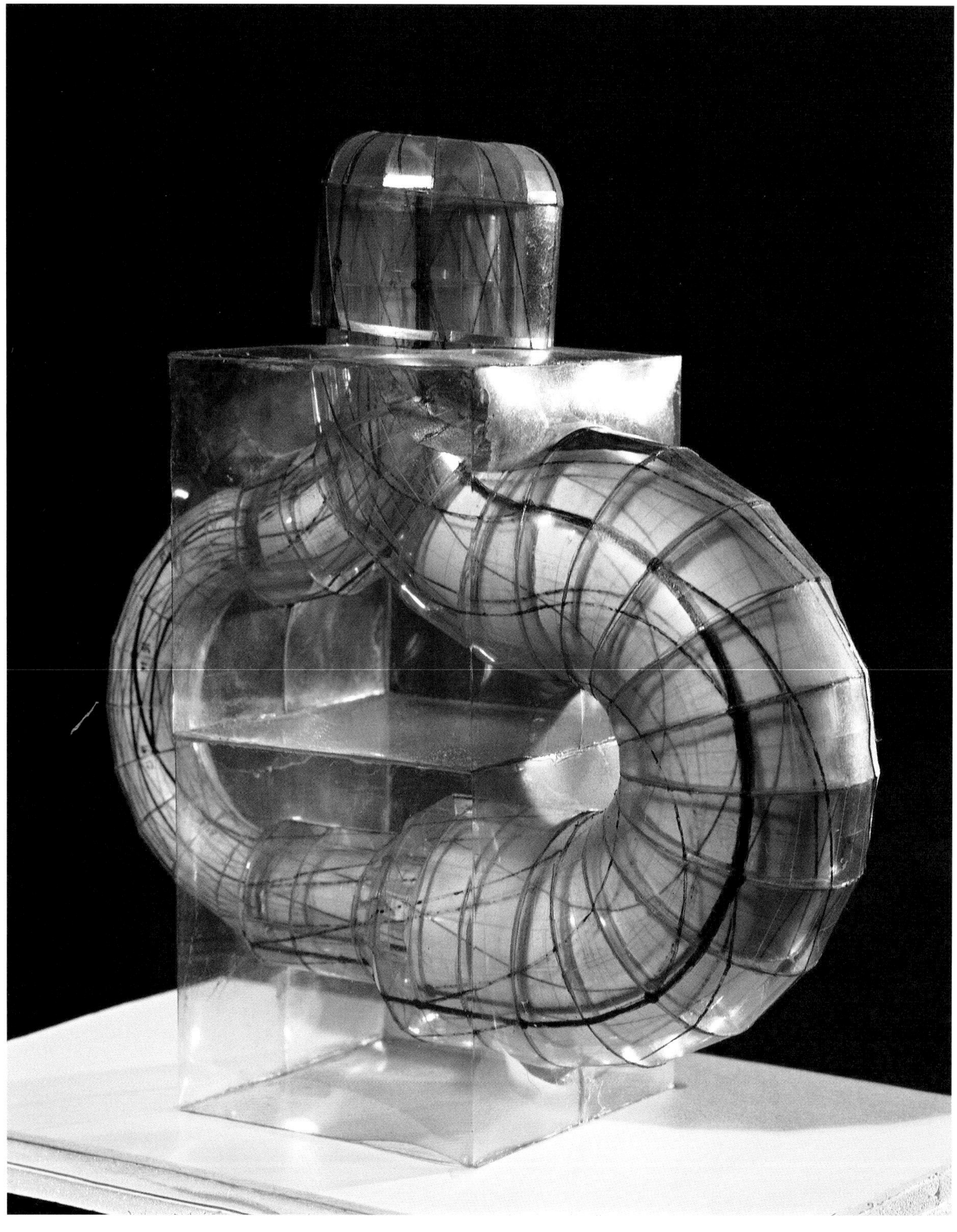

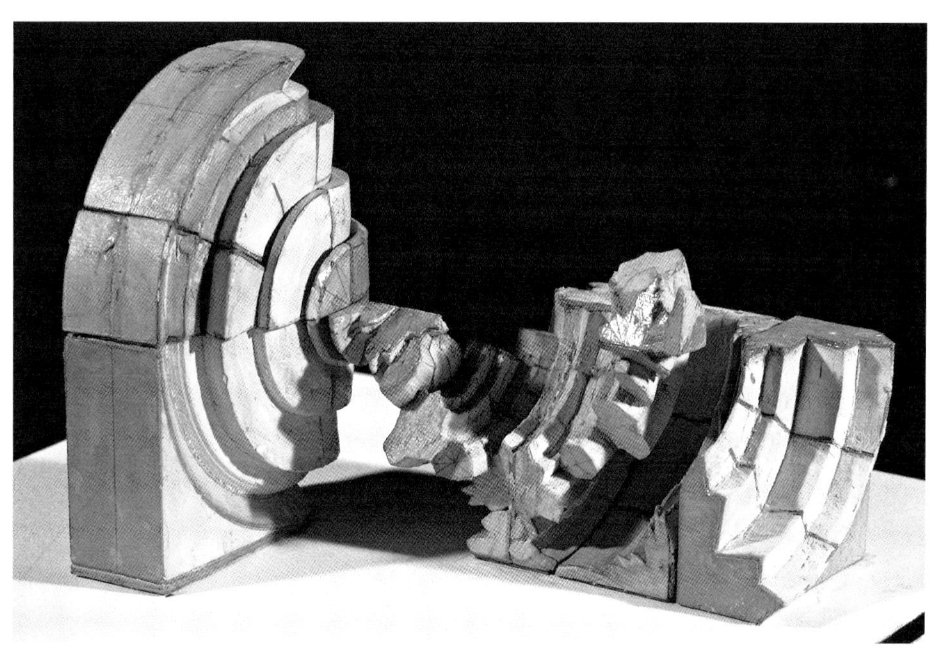

Left: Klein bottle, 1970.
Acetate, card and aluminium rim,
15 cm x 6 cm x 16 cm.
Above: Triangulation of a surface with
a spiral motion, 1965.
Plaster of Paris and card,
10 cm x 13 cm x 10 cm.

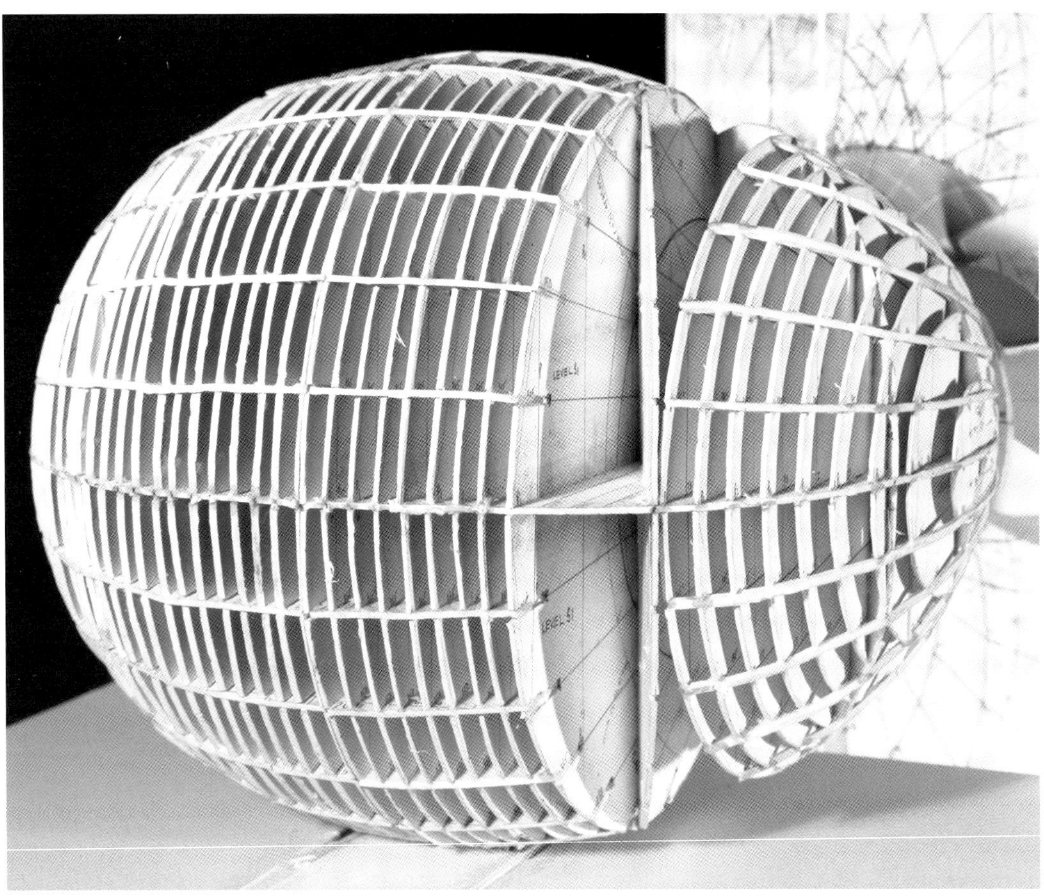

Inverting a cylinder with respect to a point not
lying on the cylinder, February–April 2002.
Card, plaster of Paris, cardboard cylinder,
65 cm x 51 cm x 56 cm.

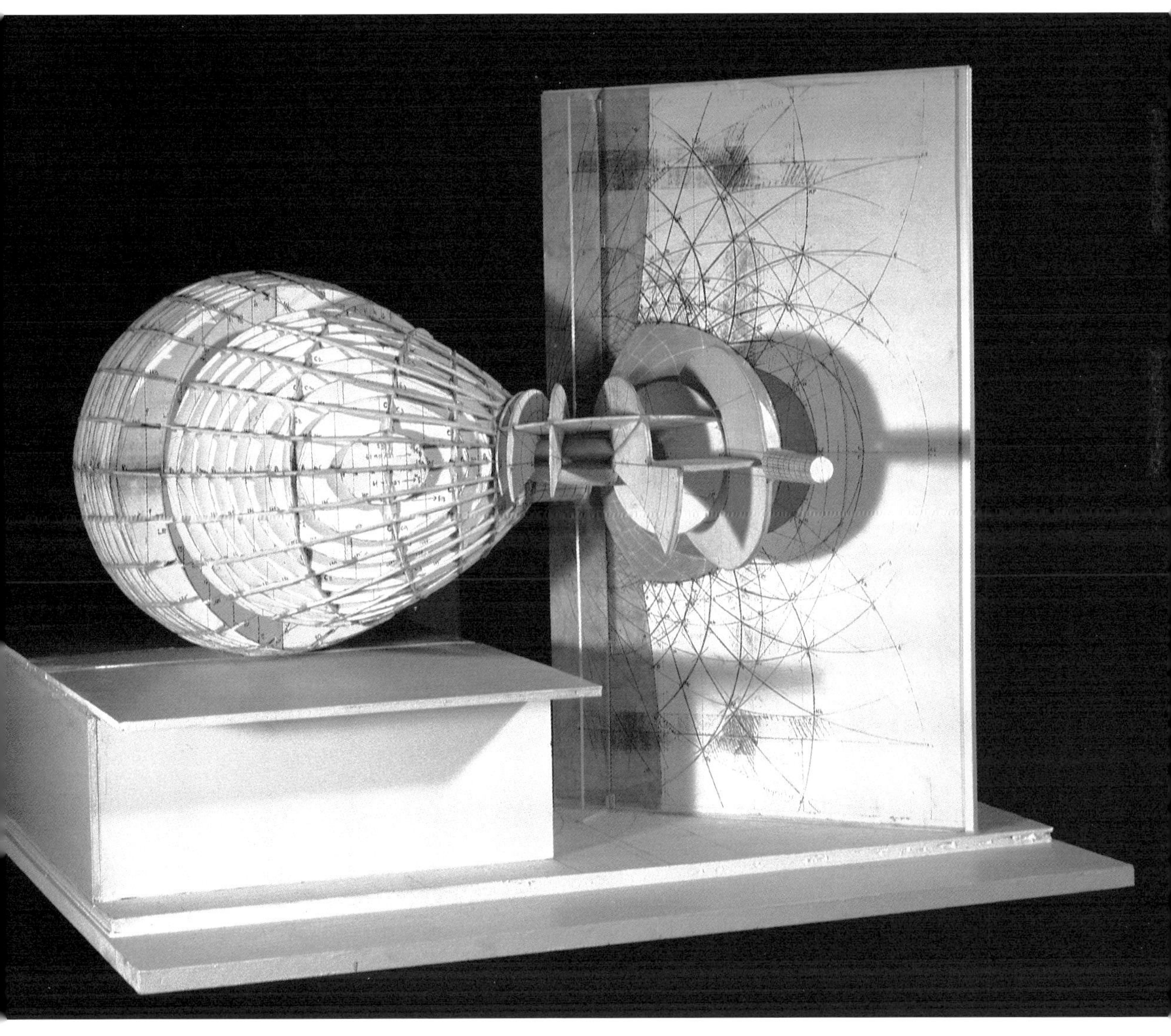

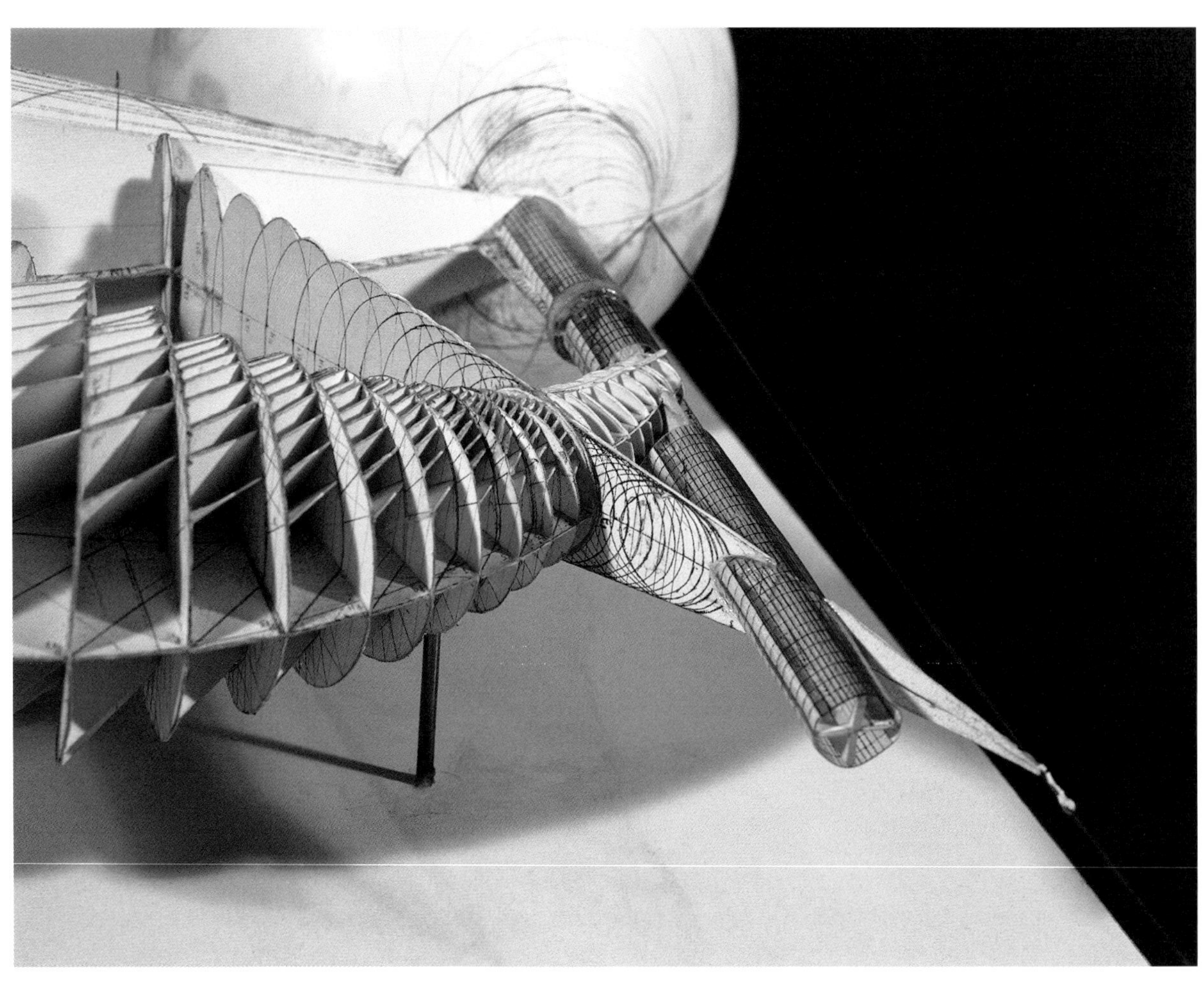

Inverting a cylinder, the centre of inversion not
lying on the cylinder, also connecting ellipses by
projection, June 1988–August 1990.
*Plaster of Paris, card, acetate cylinder, steel rods,
plastic rods*, 46 cm x 35 cm x 14 cm.

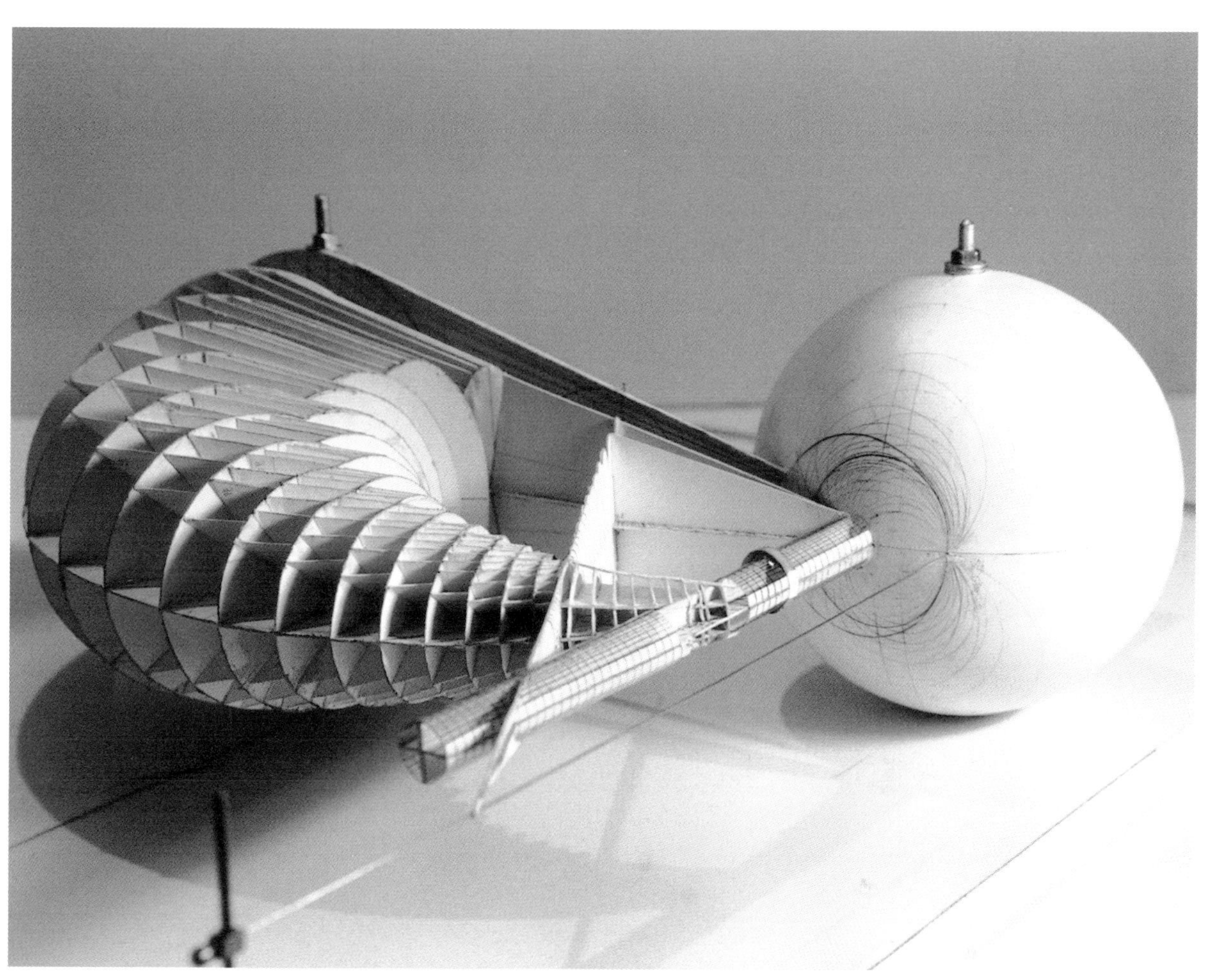

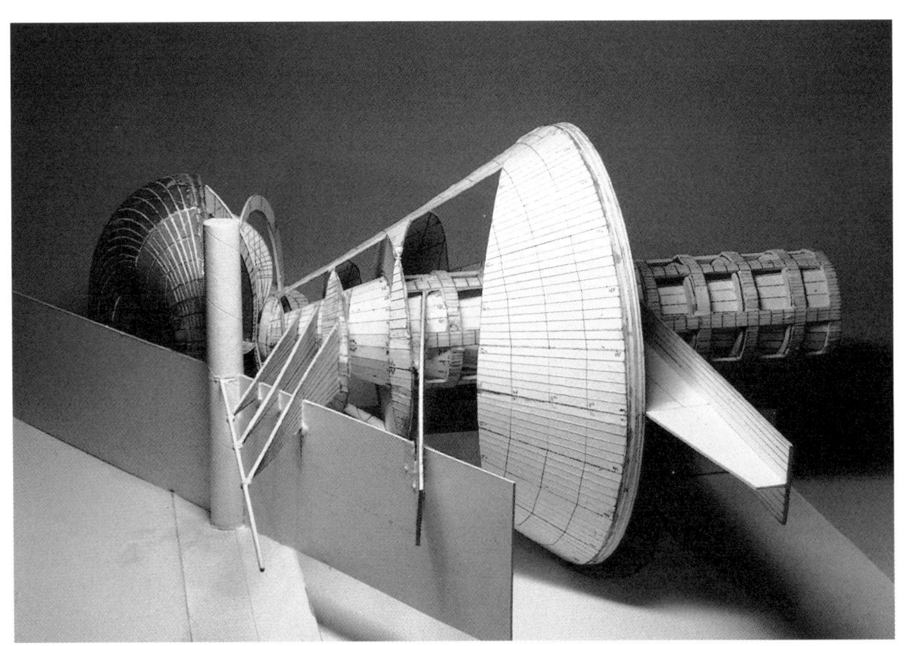

Inverting a cylinder, the centre of
inversion lying inside the cylinder,
1978–1980–1981. *Plaster of Paris and
card,* 45 cm x 43 cm x 23 cm.

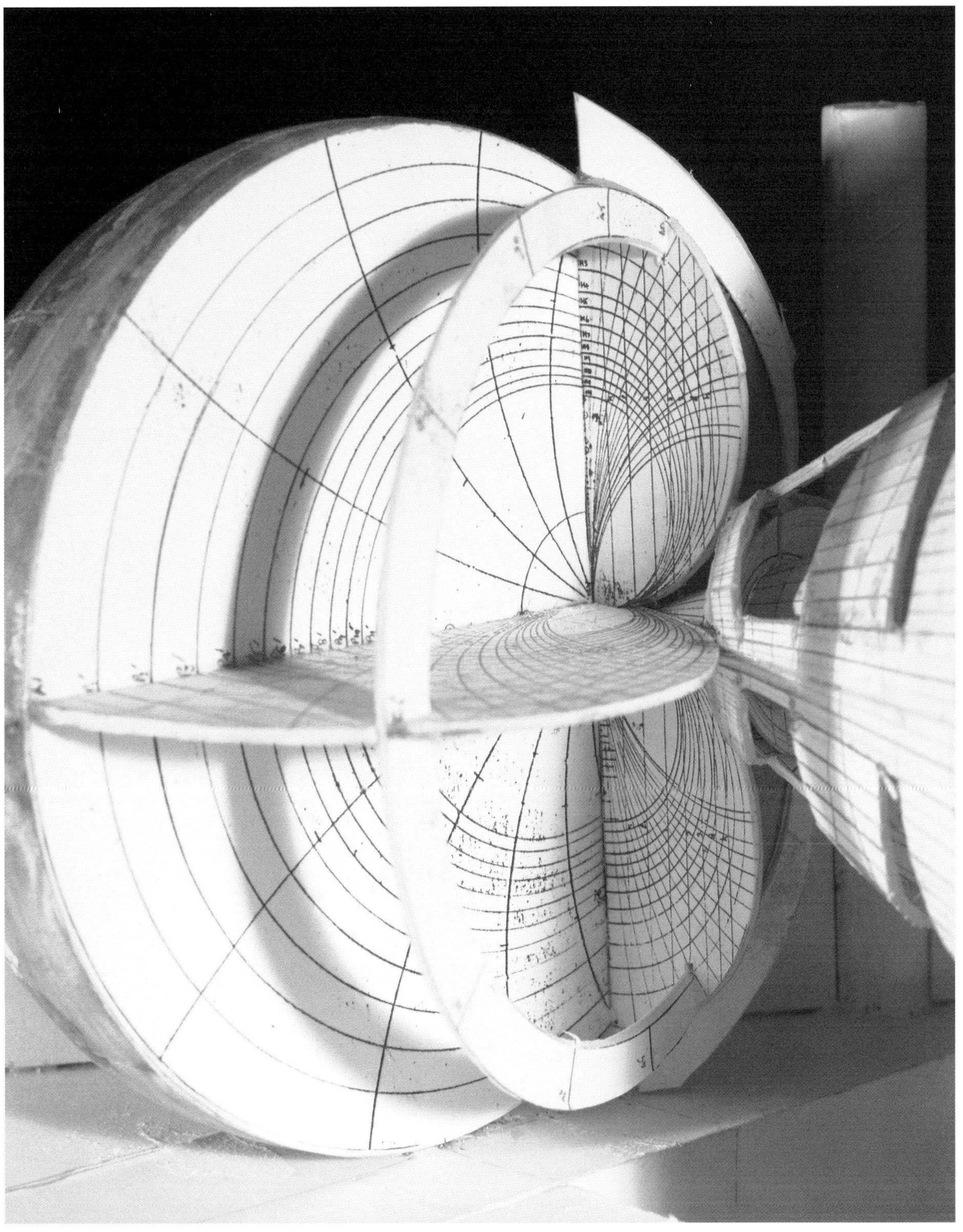

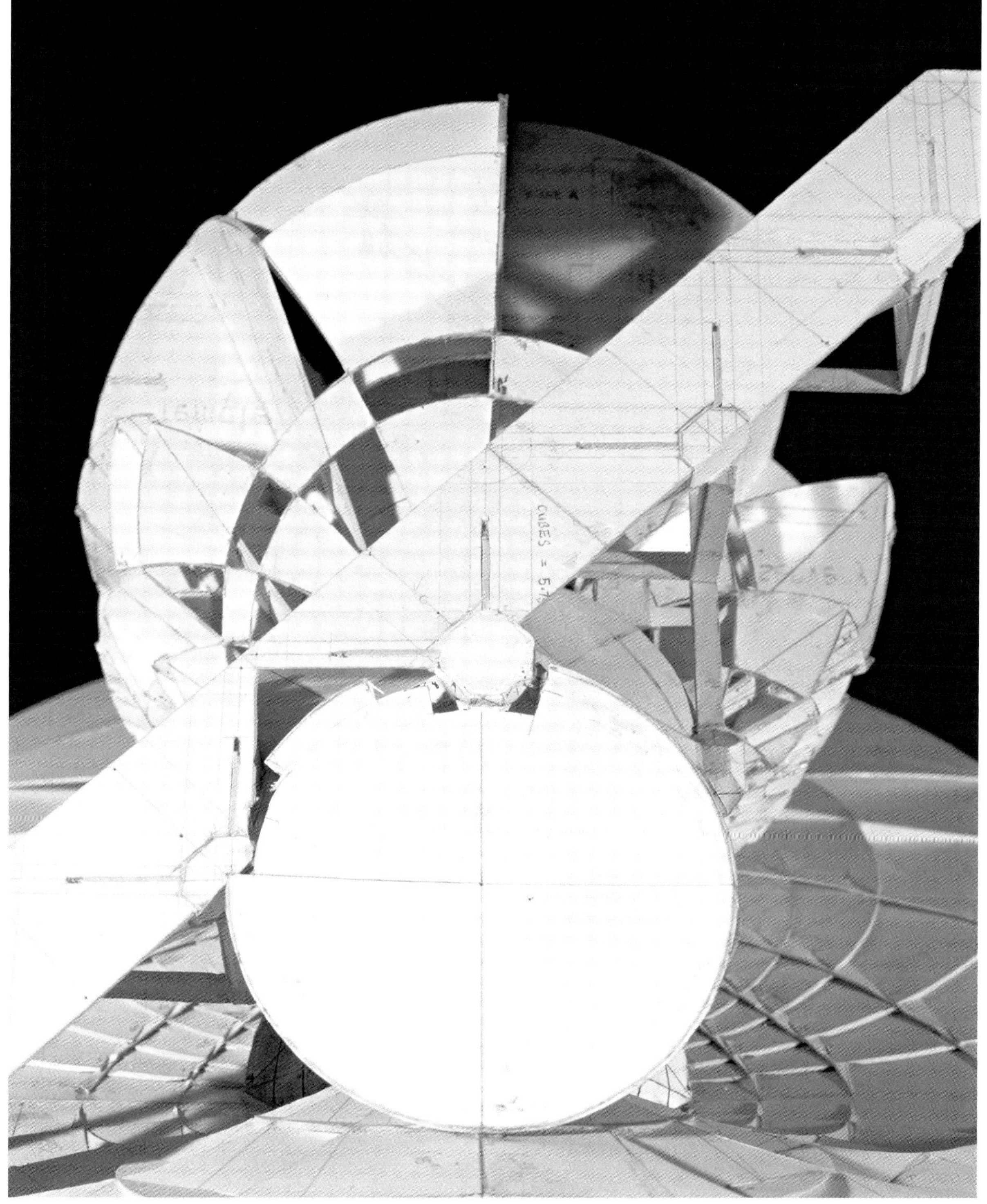

Inversion from a 90° angle cone and inversion
from a set of cubes with respect to a point not
lying on the cone or the cubes, 1976–1977.
Card, balsa wood, 88 cm x 68 cm x 30 cm.

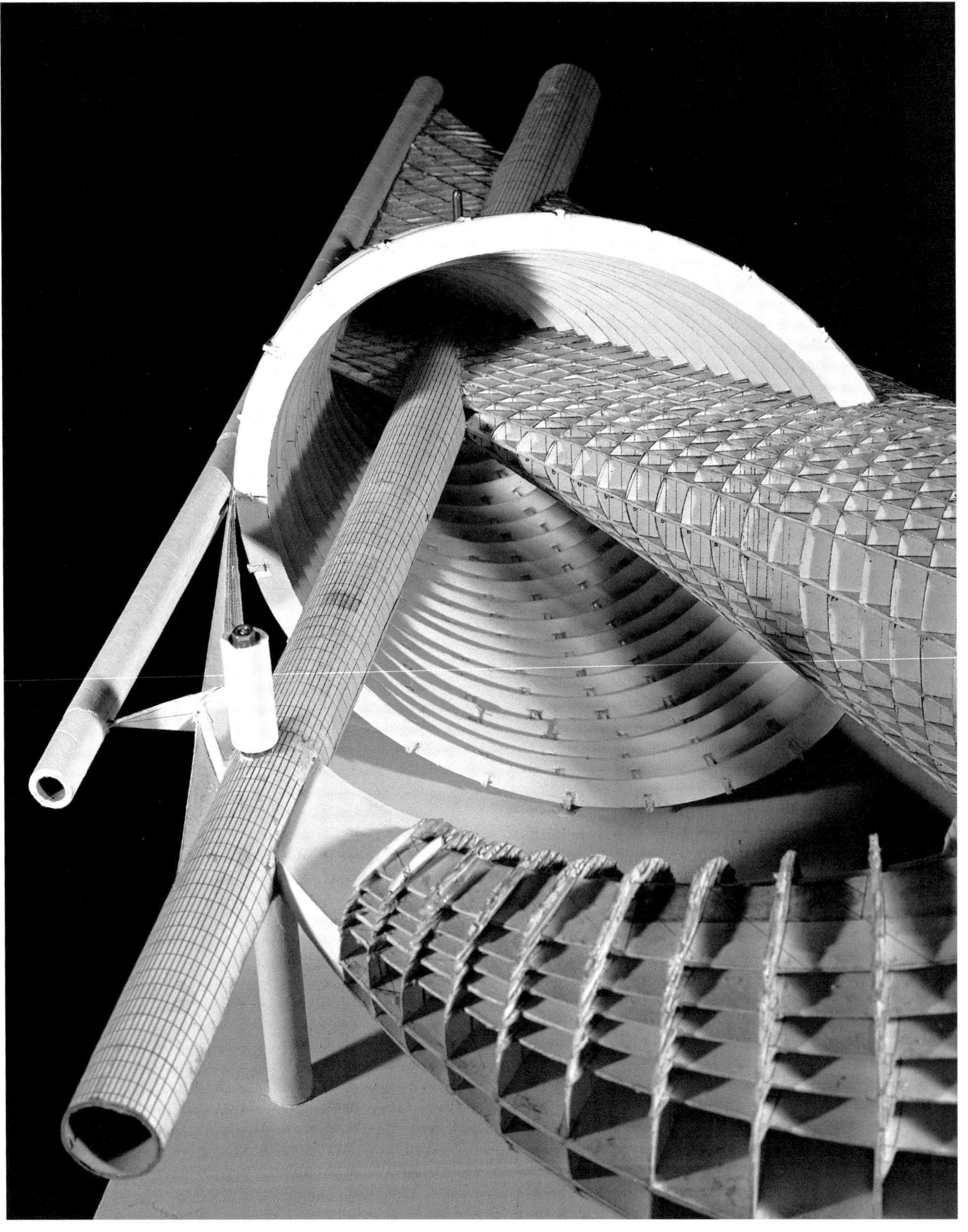

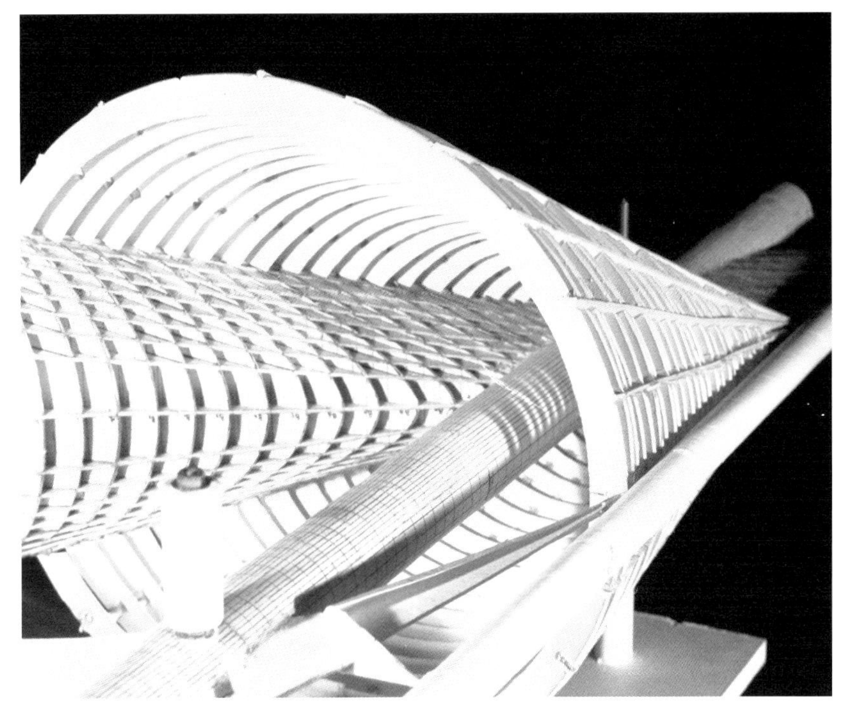

Inverting a circular cylinder where the
centre of inversion does not lie on the
cylinder, May 1992–December 1995.
*Card, cardboard cylinders, steel rod,
45 cm x 43 cm x 23 cm.*

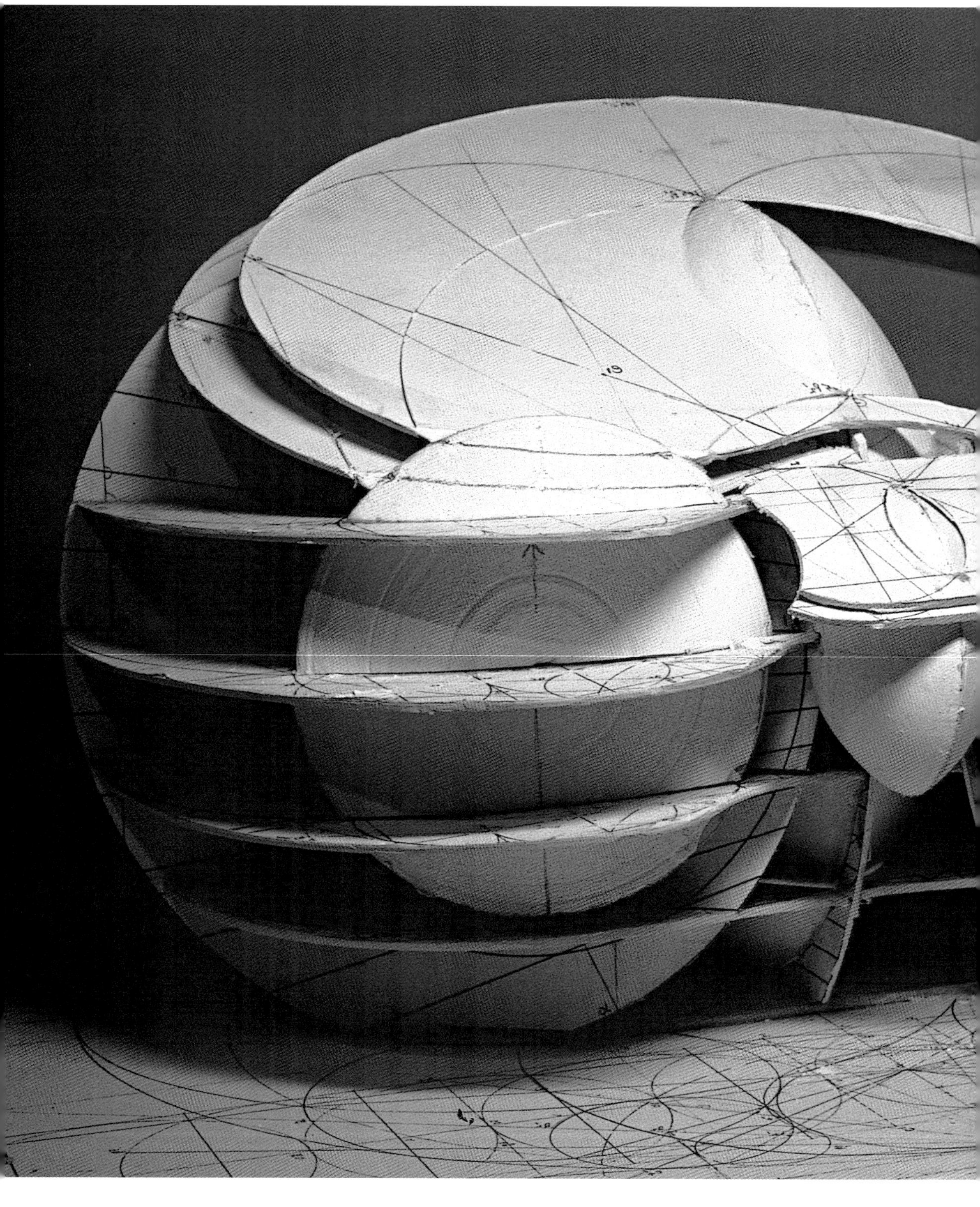

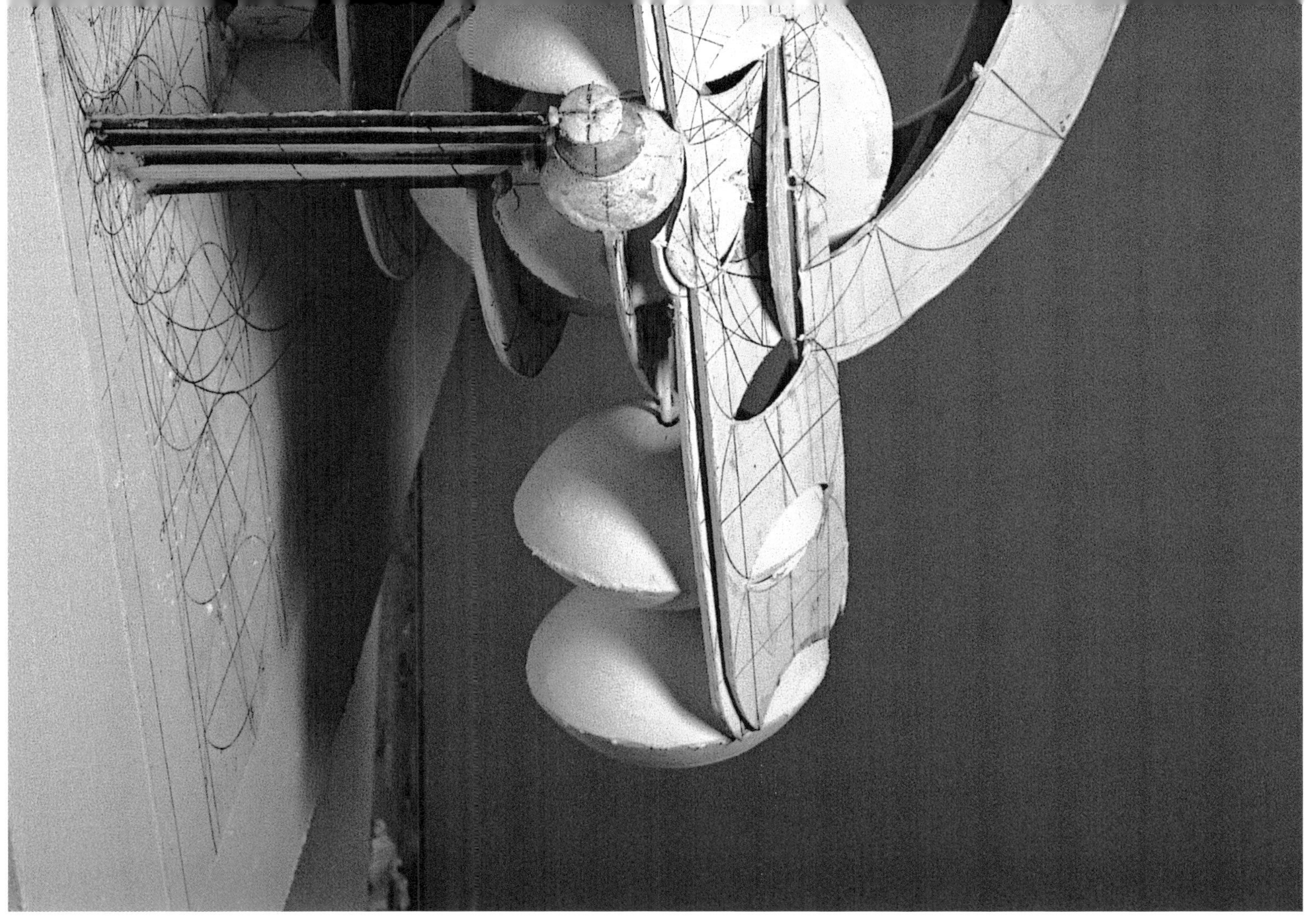

Spherical inversion. Inverting intersecting spheres whose centres lie on the axis of a cylinder, with respect to a point not lying on any of the spheres. October–December 2002.
Card, plaster of Paris, steel rods;
58 cm x 47 cm x 34 cm

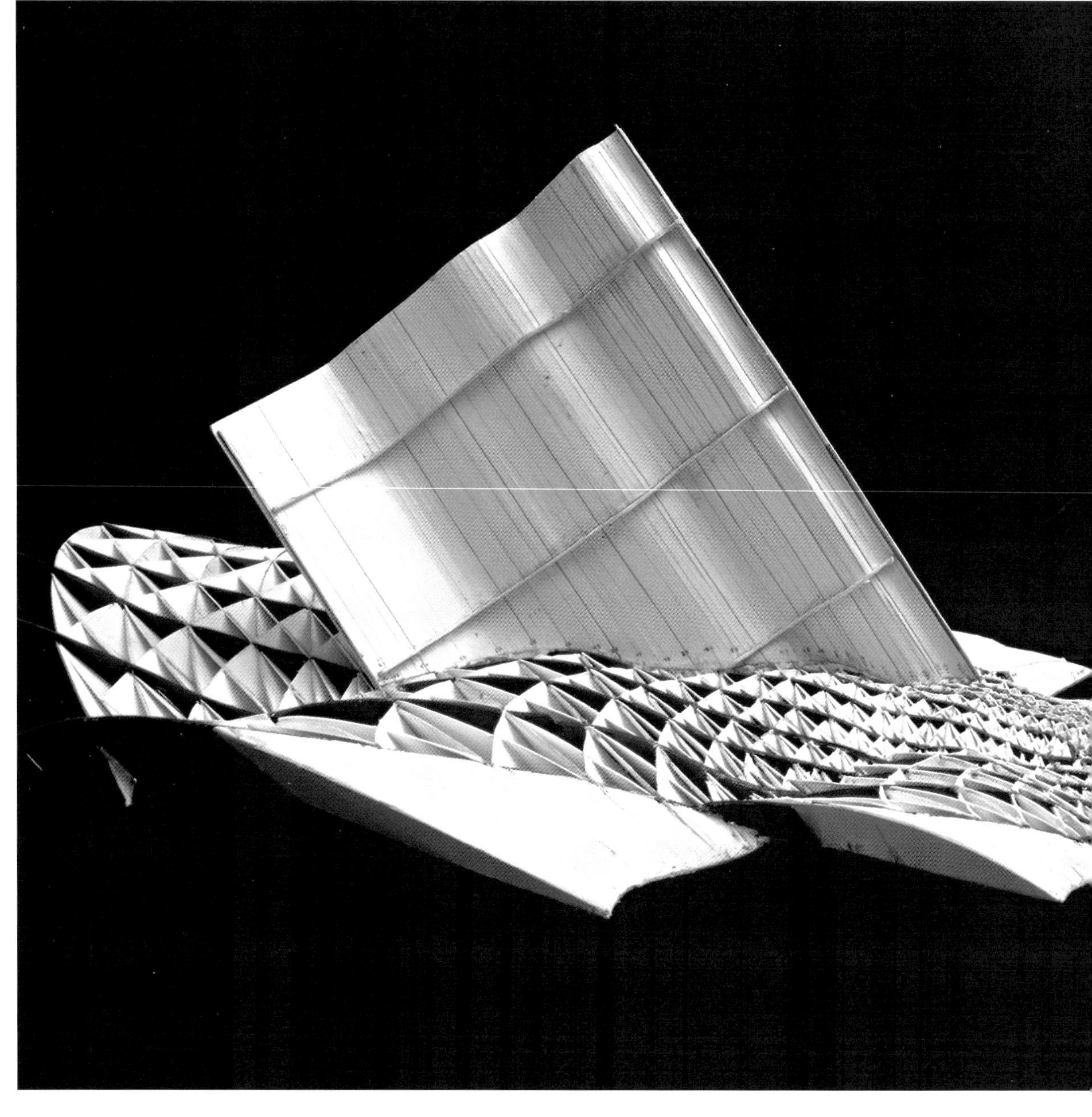

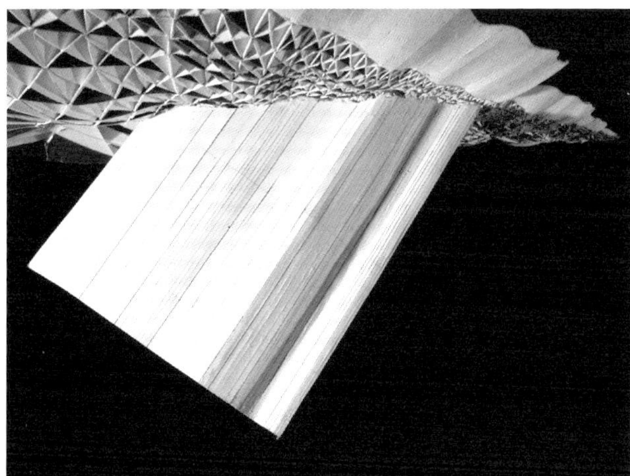

Inverting a sine wave with respect to
a point not lying on any part of the
sine wave, version 2, 2006 (two
orientations of work in progress).
Card, plaster of Paris, steel rods,
58 cm x 47 cm x 34 cm.

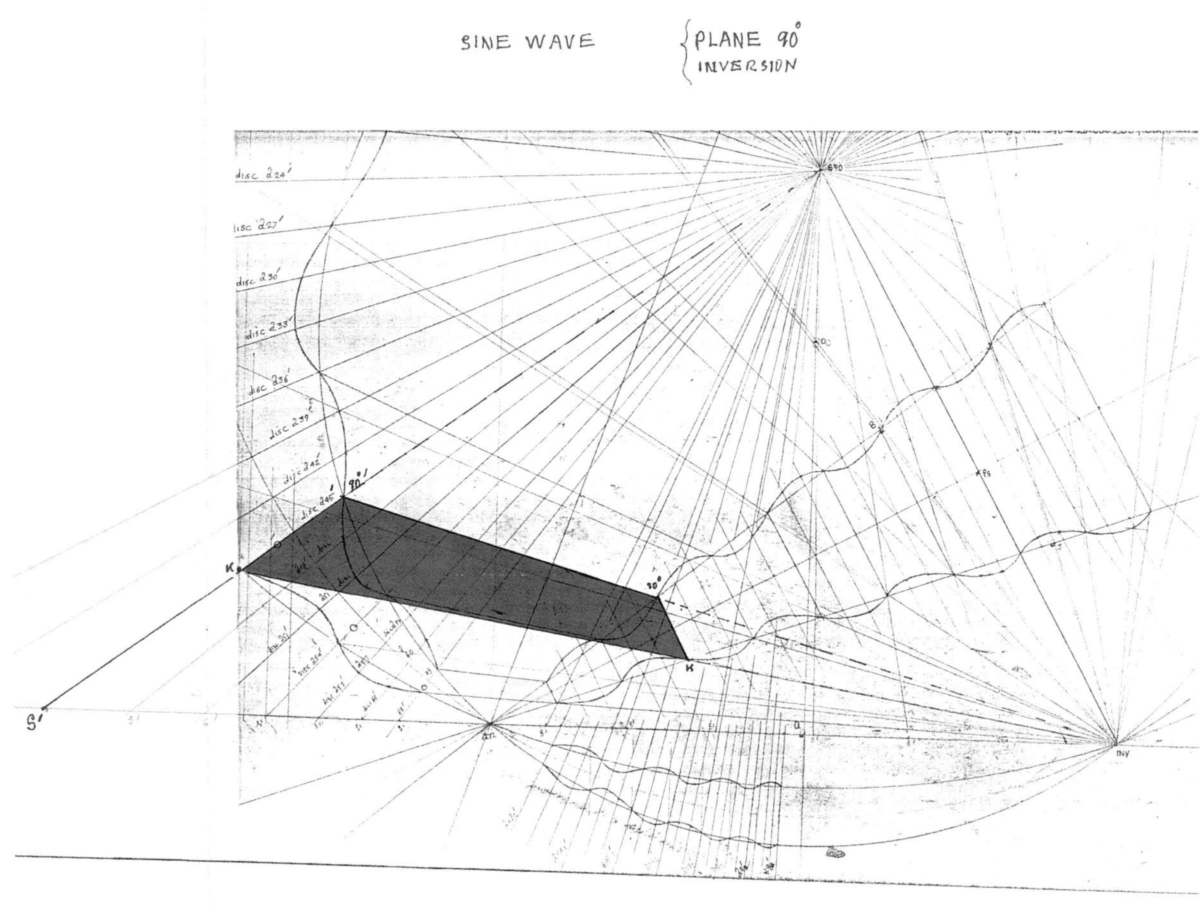

The following pages are designed to give a
hint of the process of making JP's most recent
completed work, Inverting a corrugated cone
with a sine wave profile with respect to a point not
lying on the cone or any part of the sine wave,
version 1, February 2003–October 2005.

There are six planes passing through the centre of inversion they are the main horizontal plane, plane 30°, 60°, 90°, 120° and 150°. Plane 30° assumes the ground level. If this model was developed on a grand scale everything below plane 30° could be dispensed with.

The inside surface of the undulating wave roof would mimic the exterior surface, in this model it is cut off at plane 60° to form an open structure. This form is supported by an upsidedown cone, this cone is intersected at plane 30° in an elliptic section. The cone is cut at two spirals left hand and right hand, the remaining part of the cone on plane 30° is ◢◣ and this is the base of the cone column. To fill the space below plane 30°, inversion was applied to this cone forming a cyclide.

Only part of the original sine wave structure remains. The roof part of this is plane 90°. The centres of the inversed circles of the original object are also inversed to form a wavy line on the main horizontal plane. The infinite number of points on this line are then connected to the plane 90° and this forms the dart like structure which is cut off by plane 30°.

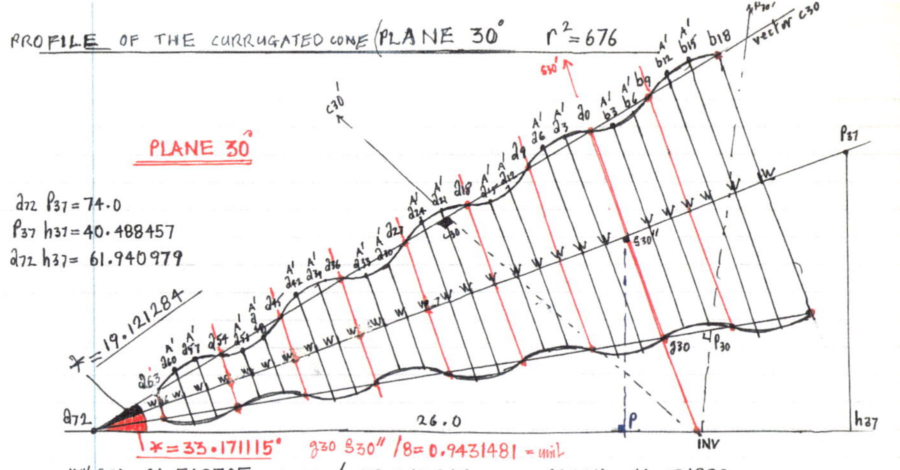

$\divideontimes = 33.171115°$ $g_{30}\ S30''/8 = 0.9431481 = unit$

INV $C30 = 20.569705$, INV $C30' = 32.863865 =$ DIAM. RADIUS $= 16.431932$

$g_{30}\ S30'' = 7.5451855 \times 2 = 15.090371 = g_{30}\ a_0$, INV $S30'' = 14.225674$, INV $g_{30} = 6.6804885$

INV $P_{30} = 6.3119082$, INV $P_{30}' = 107.09915 =$ DIAM. RADIUS $= 53.549575$

$a_{72}\ S30'' = 21.763047\ /\ 8 = 2.7203808\ /\ 3 = 0.9067936$

$S30''\ P = 11.907462$, $a_{72}\ P = 18.216546$

	distances on the w line.		WIDTHS	distances on the vector C30
	0.9067936			0.9597453
a_{72} W	1.8135872	$a_{72}A' = 1.8681543$		1.9194907
a_{72} W	2.7203808		$a_{63}w' = 0.9431481 \times 2 = 1.8862964$	2.879236
a_{72} W	3.6271744	$a_{72}A' = 3.899992$	$a_{60}A'w = 1.433019 \times 2 = 2.866038$	3.8389813
a_{72} W	4.533968	$a_{72}A' = 4.8715545$	$A'a_{57}w = 1.7819027 \times 2 = 3.5638055$	4.7987267
a_{72} W	5.4407616		$a_{54}w = 1.8862964 \times 2 = 3.7725927$	5.758472
a_{72} W	6.3475552	$a_{72}A' = 6.6516039$	$A'a_{51}w = 1.9880587 \times 2 = 3.9761174$	6.7182173
a_{72} W	7.2543488	$a_{72}A' = 7.6216785$	$A'a_{48}w = 2.337607 \times 2 = 4.675214$	7.6779626
a_{72} W	8.1611424		$a_{45}w = 2.8294446 \times 2 = 5.6588891$	8.637708
a_{72} W	9.067936	$a_{72}A' = 9.6566028$	$A'a_{42}w = 3.3200172 \times 2 = 6.6400344$	9.5974533
a W	9.9747296	$a_{72}A' = 10.628082$	$A'a_{39}w = 3.6689094 \times 2 = 7.3378187$	10.557199
a_{72} W	10.881523		$a_{36}w = 3.7725927 \times 2 = 7.5451854$	11.516944
a_{72} W	11.788317	$a_{72}A' = 12.398345$	$A'a_{33}w = 3.841164 \times 2 = 7.682328$	12.476689
a_{72} W	12.69511	$a_{72}A' = 13.379463$	$A'a_{30}w = 4.2242411 \times 2 = 8.4484822$	13.436435
a_{72} W	13.601904		$a_{27}w = 4.7157409 \times 2 = 9.4314819$	14.39618
a_{72} W	14.508698	$a_{72}A' = 15.41461$	$A'a_{24}w = 5.2065232 \times 2 = 10.413046$	15.355926
a_{72} W	15.415491	$a_{72}A' = 16.38597$	$A'a_{21}w = 5.5554163 \times 2 = 11.110833$	16.315671
a_{72} W	16.322285		$a_{18}w = 5.6588892 \times 2 = 11.317778$	17.275416
a_{72} W	17.229078	$a_{72}A' = 18.16688$	$A'a_{15}w = 5.7614581 \times 2 = 11.522916$	18.235162
a_{72} W	18.135872	$a_{72}A' = 19.137226$	$A'a_{12}w = 6.1093015 \times 2 = 12.218603$	19.194907
a_{72} W	19.042666		$a_9w = 6.6020375 \times 2 = 13.204075$	20.154652
a_{72} W	19.949459	$a_{72}A' = 21.172859$	$A'a_6w = 7.0928869 \times 2 = 14.185774$	21.114397
a_{72} W	20.856253	$a_{72}A' = 22.14418$	$A'a_3w = 7.4418693 \times 2 = 14.883739$	22.074143
a_{72} S30''	21.763046		$a_0w = 7.5451854 \times 2 = 15.090371$	23.033888
a_{72} W	22.66984	$a_{72}A' = 23.900471$	$A'b_3w = 7.5703942 \times 2 = 15.140788$	23.993633
a_{72} W	23.576634	$a_{72}A' = 24.895985$	$A'b_6w = 7.9970244 \times 2 = 15.994049$	24.953379
a_{72} W	24.483427		$b_9w = 8.4883336 \times 2 = 16.976667$	25.913124
a_{72} W	25.390221	$a_{72}A' = 26.931211$	$A'b_{12}w = 8.9792429 \times 2 = 17.958486$	26.872869
a_{72} W	26.297014	$a_{72}A' = 27.906254$	$A'b_{15}w = 9.3394897 \times 2 = 18.678979$	27.832615
a_{72} W	27.203808		$b_{18}w = 9.4314819 \times 2 = 18.862964$	28.79236

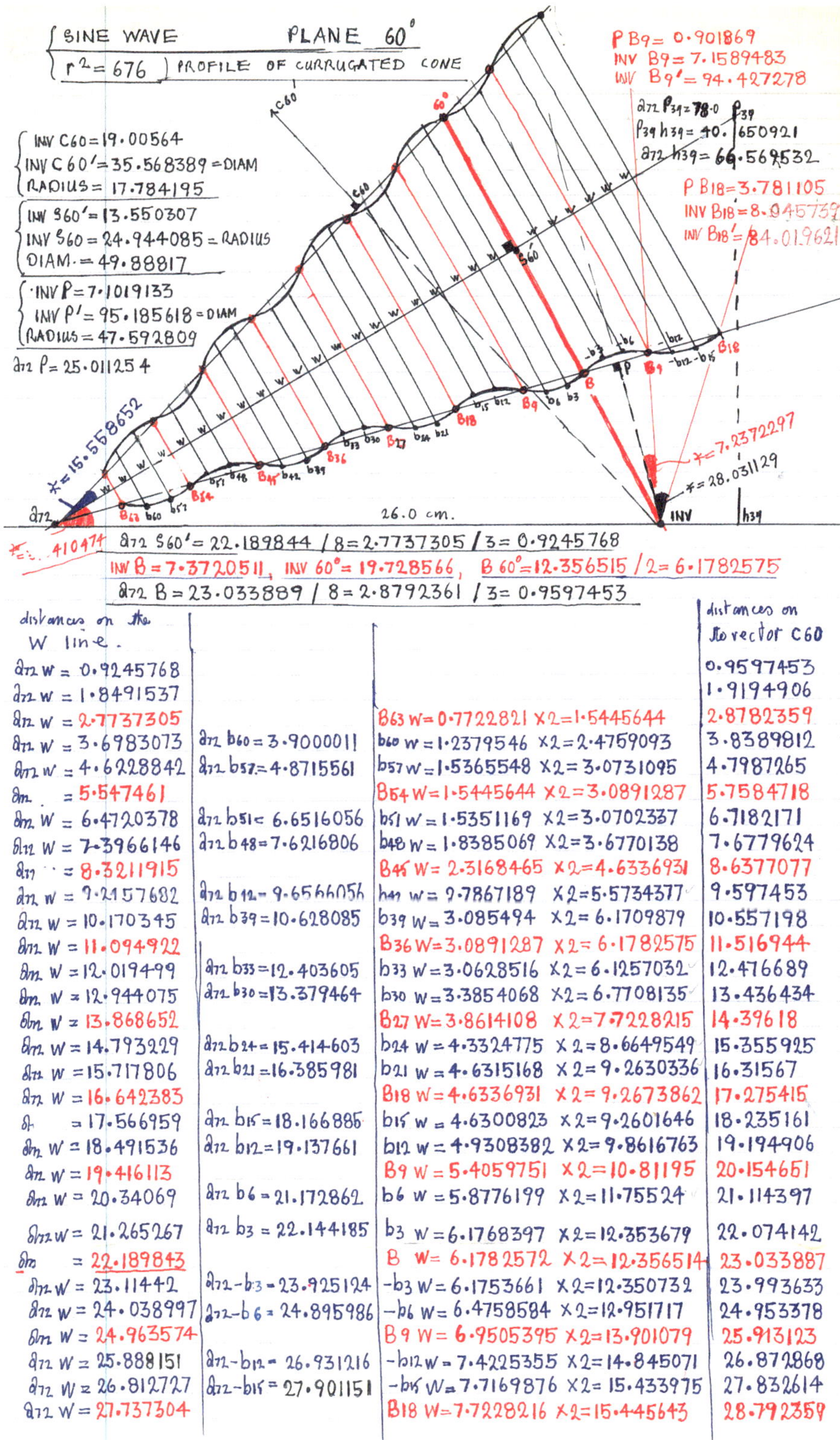

SINE WAVE   PLANE 60°
r² = 676   PROFILE OF CURRUGATED CONE

INV C60 = 19.00564
INV C60' = 35.568389 = DIAM
RADIUS = 17.784195

INV S60' = 13.550307
INV S60 = 24.944085 = RADIUS
DIAM. = 49.88817

INV P = 7.1019133
INV P' = 95.185618 = DIAM
RADIUS = 47.592809

∂72 P = 25.011254

x = 15.558652
∂72
x = ..410474

C60
60°

P B9 = 0.901869
INV B9 = 7.1589483
INV B9' = 94.427278

∂72 P39 = 78.0   P39
P39 h39 = 40.650921
∂72 h39 = 66.569532

P B18 = 3.781105
INV B18 = 8.9457597
INV B18' = 84.019621

x = 7.2372297
x = 28.031129

26.0 cm.
INV   h39

∂72 S60' = 22.189844 / 8 = 2.7737305 / 3 = 0.9245768
INV B = 7.3720511,   INV 60° = 19.728566,   B 60° = 12.356515 / 2 = 6.1782575
∂72 B = 23.033889 / 8 = 2.8792361 / 3 = 0.9597453

distances on the W line.
∂72 W = 0.9245768
∂72 W = 1.8491537
∂72 W = 2.7737305
∂72 W = 3.6983073
∂72 W = 4.6228842
∂m   = 5.547461
∂m W = 6.4720378
∂72 W = 7.3966146
∂72 = 8.3211915
∂72 W = 9.2157682
∂72 W = 10.170345
∂72 W = 11.094922
∂m W = 12.019499
∂m W = 12.944075
∂m W = 13.868652
∂m W = 14.793229
∂72 W = 15.717806
∂72 W = 16.642383
∂ = 17.566959
∂m W = 18.491536
∂m W = 19.416113
∂72 W = 20.34069
∂72 W = 21.265267
∂m = 22.189843
∂72 W = 23.11442
∂72 W = 24.038997
∂m W = 24.963574
∂72 W = 25.888151
∂72 W = 26.812727
∂72 W = 27.737304

∂72 b60 = 3.9000011
∂72 b57 = 4.8715561
∂72 b51 = 6.6516056
∂72 b48 = 7.6216806
∂72 b42 = 9.6566056
∂72 b39 = 10.628085
∂72 b33 = 12.403605
∂72 b30 = 13.379464
∂72 b24 = 15.414603
∂72 b21 = 16.385981
∂72 b15 = 18.166885
∂72 b12 = 19.137661
∂72 b6 = 21.172862
∂72 b3 = 22.144185
∂72 -b3 = 23.925124
∂72 -b6 = 24.895986
∂72 -b12 = 26.931216
∂72 -b15 = 27.901151

B63 W = 0.7722821 X2 = 1.5445644
b60 w = 1.2379546 X2 = 2.4759093
b57 w = 1.5365548 X2 = 3.0731095
B54 W = 1.5445644 X2 = 3.0891287
b51 w = 1.5351169 X2 = 3.0702337
b48 w = 1.8385069 X2 = 3.6770138
B45 W = 2.3168465 X2 = 4.6336931
h42 w = 2.7867189 X2 = 5.5734377
b39 w = 3.085494   X2 = 6.1709879
B36 W = 3.0891287 X2 = 6.1782575
b33 w = 3.0628516 X2 = 6.1257032
b30 w = 3.3854068 X2 = 6.7708135
B27 W = 3.8614108 X2 = 7.7228215
b24 w = 4.3324775 X2 = 8.6649549
b21 w = 4.6315168 X2 = 9.2630336
B18 W = 4.6336931 X2 = 9.2673862
b15 w = 4.6300823 X2 = 9.2601646
b12 w = 4.9308382 X2 = 9.8616763
B9 W = 5.4059751   X2 = 10.81195
b6 w = 5.8776199   X2 = 11.75524
b3 W = 6.1768397   X2 = 12.353679
B W = 6.1782572   X2 = 12.356514
-b3 W = 6.1753661 X2 = 12.350732
-b6 W = 6.4758584 X2 = 12.951717
B9 W = 6.9505395   X2 = 13.901079
-b12 W = 7.4225355 X2 = 14.845071
-b15 W = 7.7169876 X2 = 15.433975
B18 W = 7.7228216 X2 = 15.445643

distances on to vector C60
0.9597453
1.9194906
2.8782359
3.8389812
4.7987265
5.7584718
6.7182171
7.6779624
8.6377077
9.597453
10.557198
11.516944
12.476689
13.436434
14.39618
15.355925
16.31567
17.275415
18.235161
19.194906
20.154651
21.114397
22.074142
23.033887
23.993633
24.953378
25.913123
26.872868
27.832614
28.792359

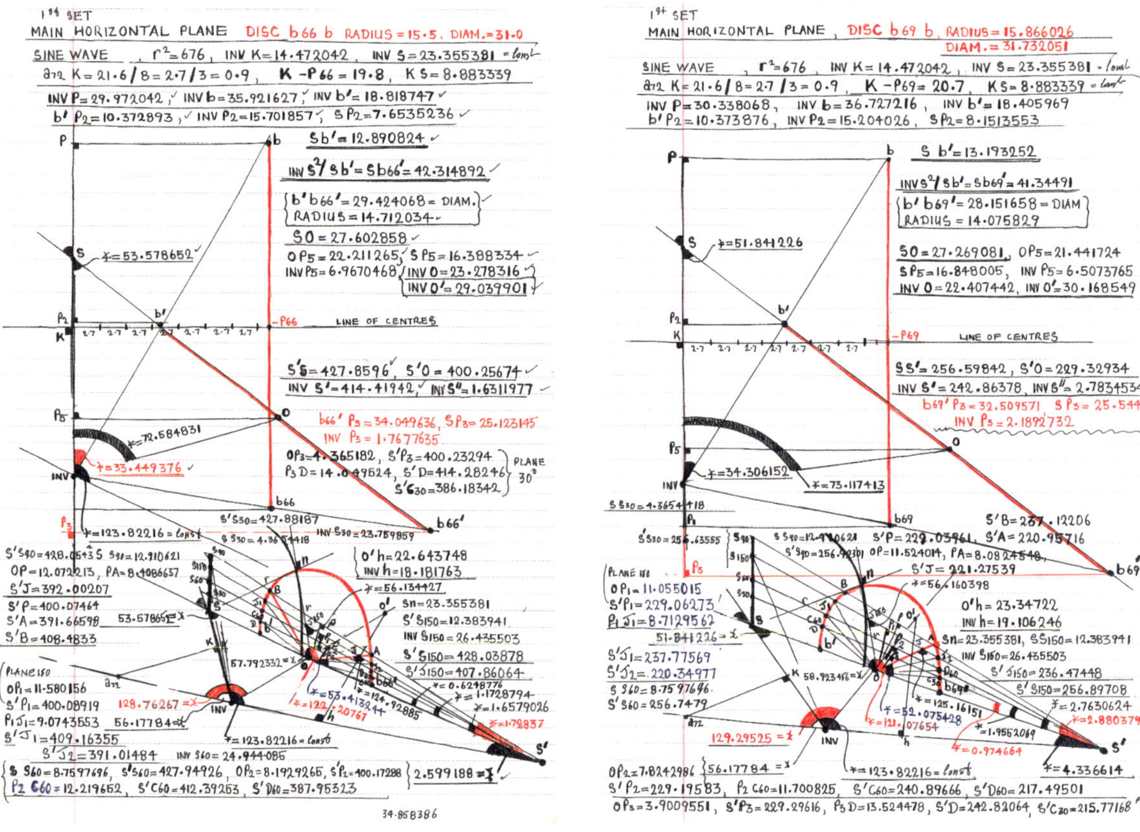

Page 66: The sine wave profiles are in arithmetic progression. adding the number 3 each time. The sine wave crosses the two straight lines with vertex 272: these straight lines are inverted into circles which pass through the centre of inversion INV. Each of the inverted sine waves weaves in and out of each circle every third segment.

Page 67: Finding the chord widths between two sine waves on plane 60°. Inverting the two straight lines that meet at vertex 272 into circles with diameters INV C60' and INV P'. Each of the inverted sine waves weaves in and out of each circle every third segment.

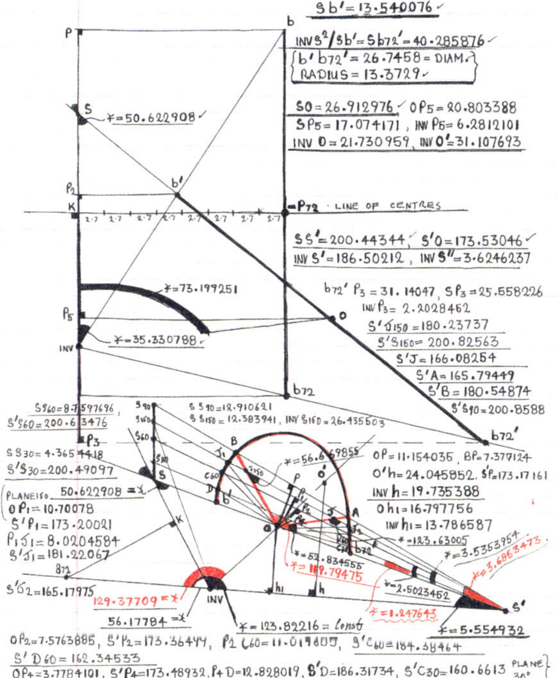

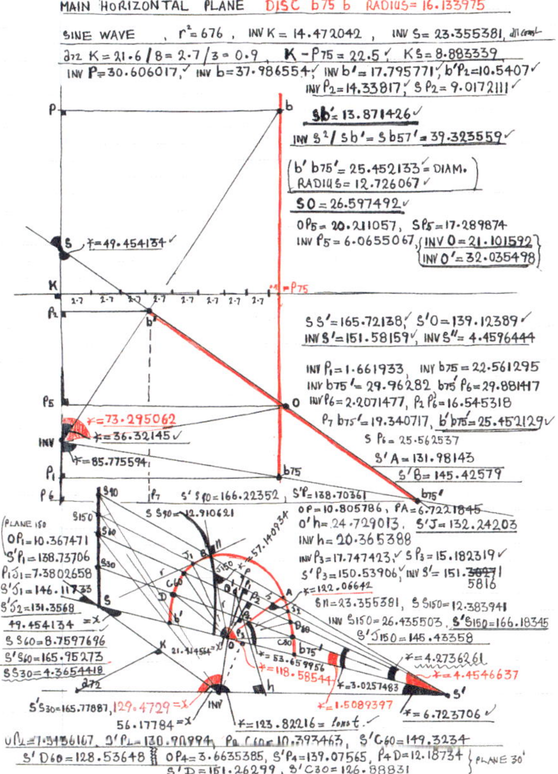

Above: Inverting the disc sections of the corrugated cone with a sine wave profile. Fixing the planes 30°, 60°, 150° and 90° produced from S' onto the vertical line S, inverting the centres of each inverted disc to O'.

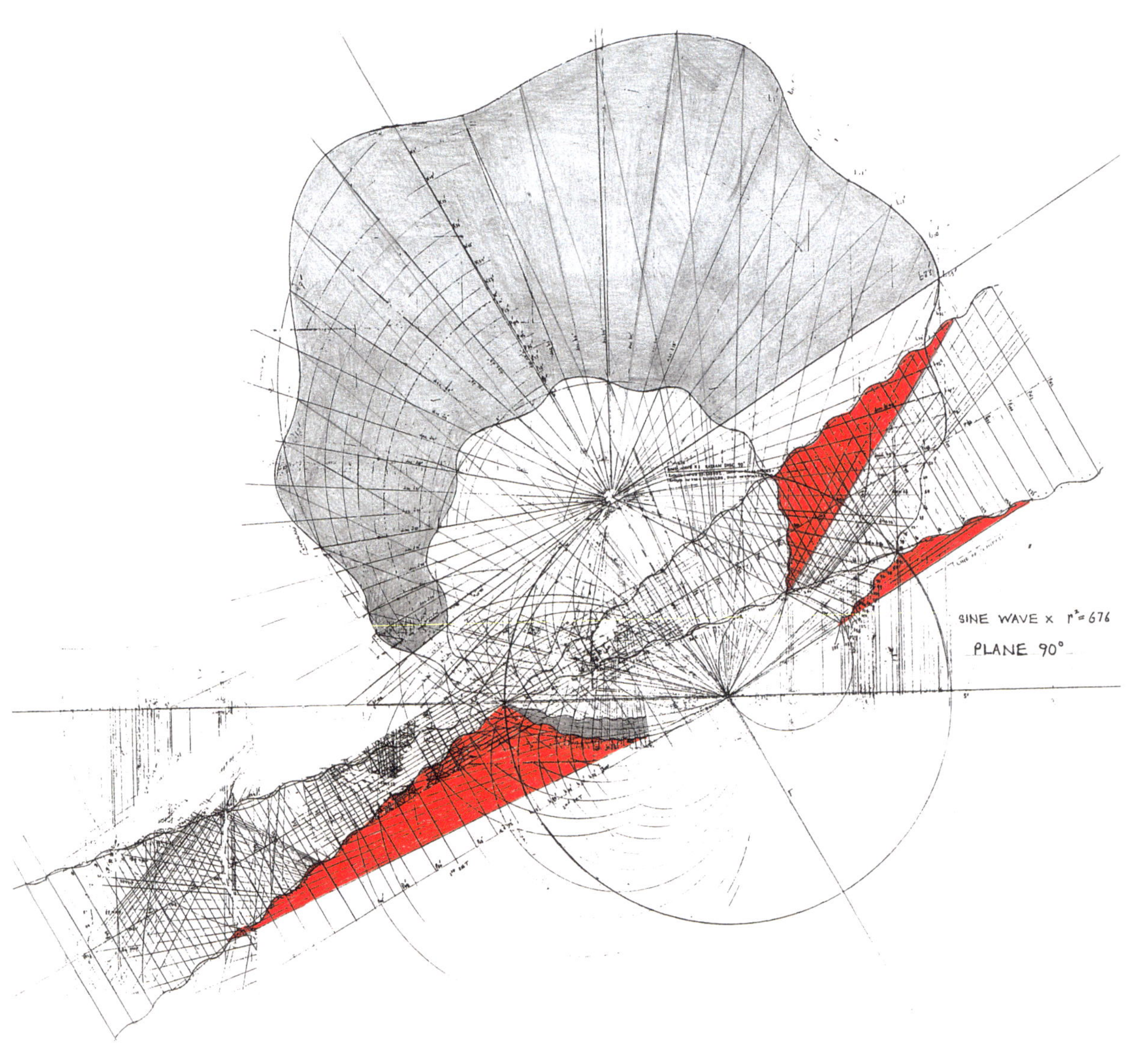

This and following spread: Inversed mappings on the 90°, 150° and main horizontal planes. The red-stained areas are parts of a sine wave and its inverse. The red areas and the projective lines form the centre of inversion.

Analogous to these stained areas is the bursting of the capillary vessels just beneath the surface of the skin – a reference to JP's experience with rheumatoid arthritis and the side-effects of taking steroid medication over many years.

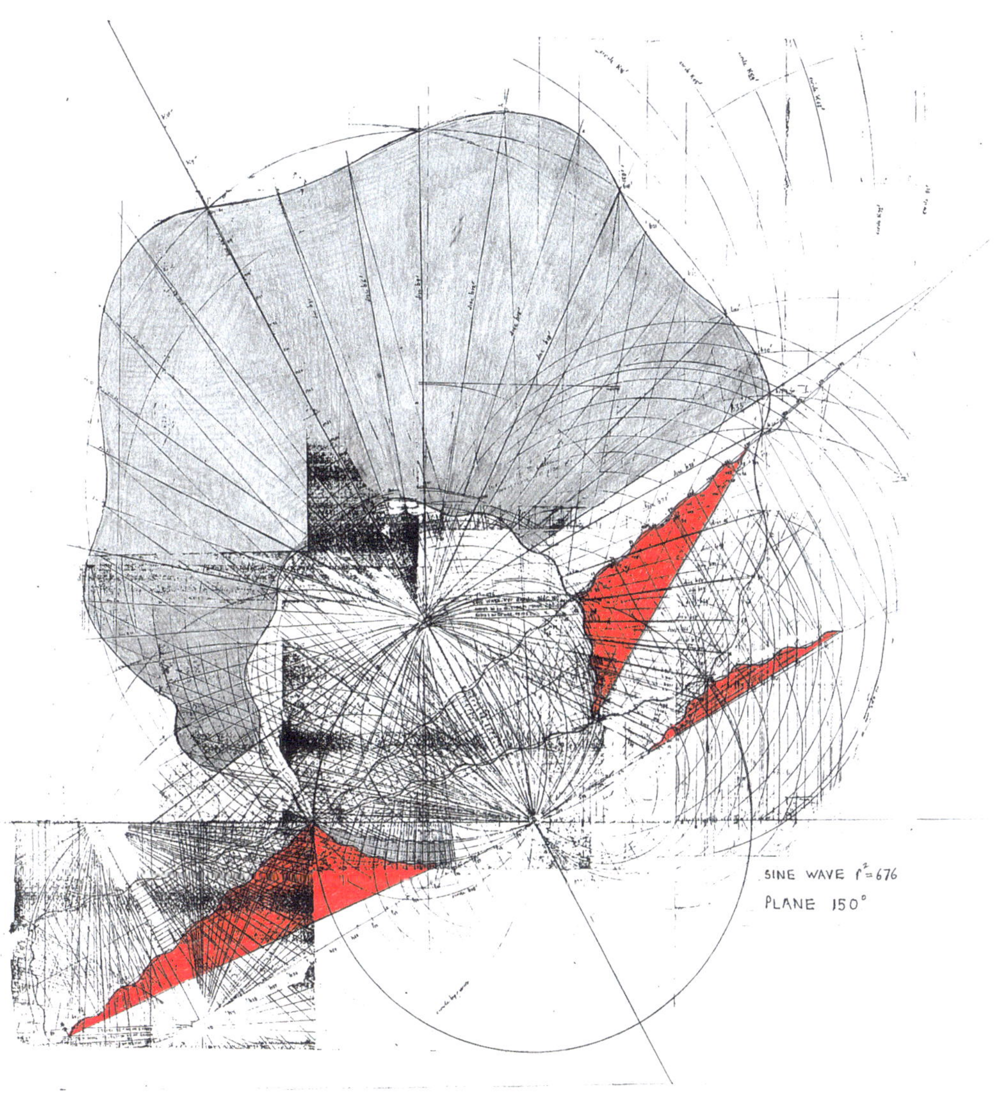

SINE WAVE r² = 676
PLANE 150°

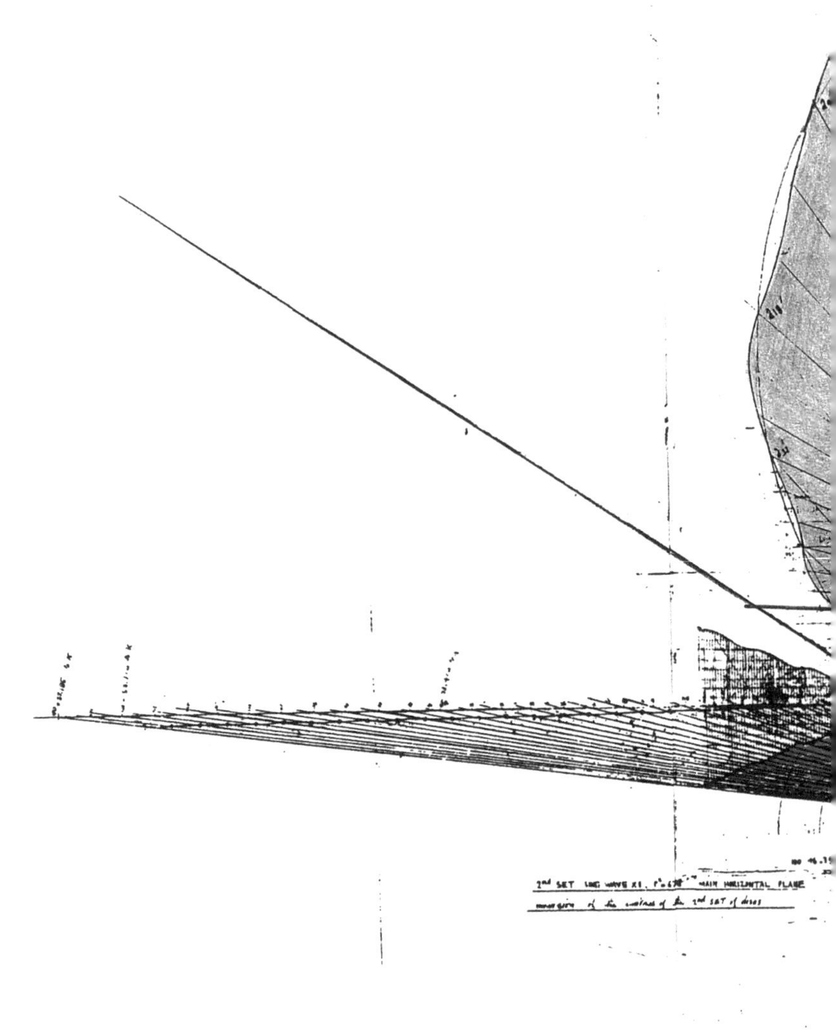

A symbolic reflection to this cone and its inverse,
the cyclide, is Mantegna's *The Martyrdom of
St Sebastian*, with its vector arrows of projective
geometry.

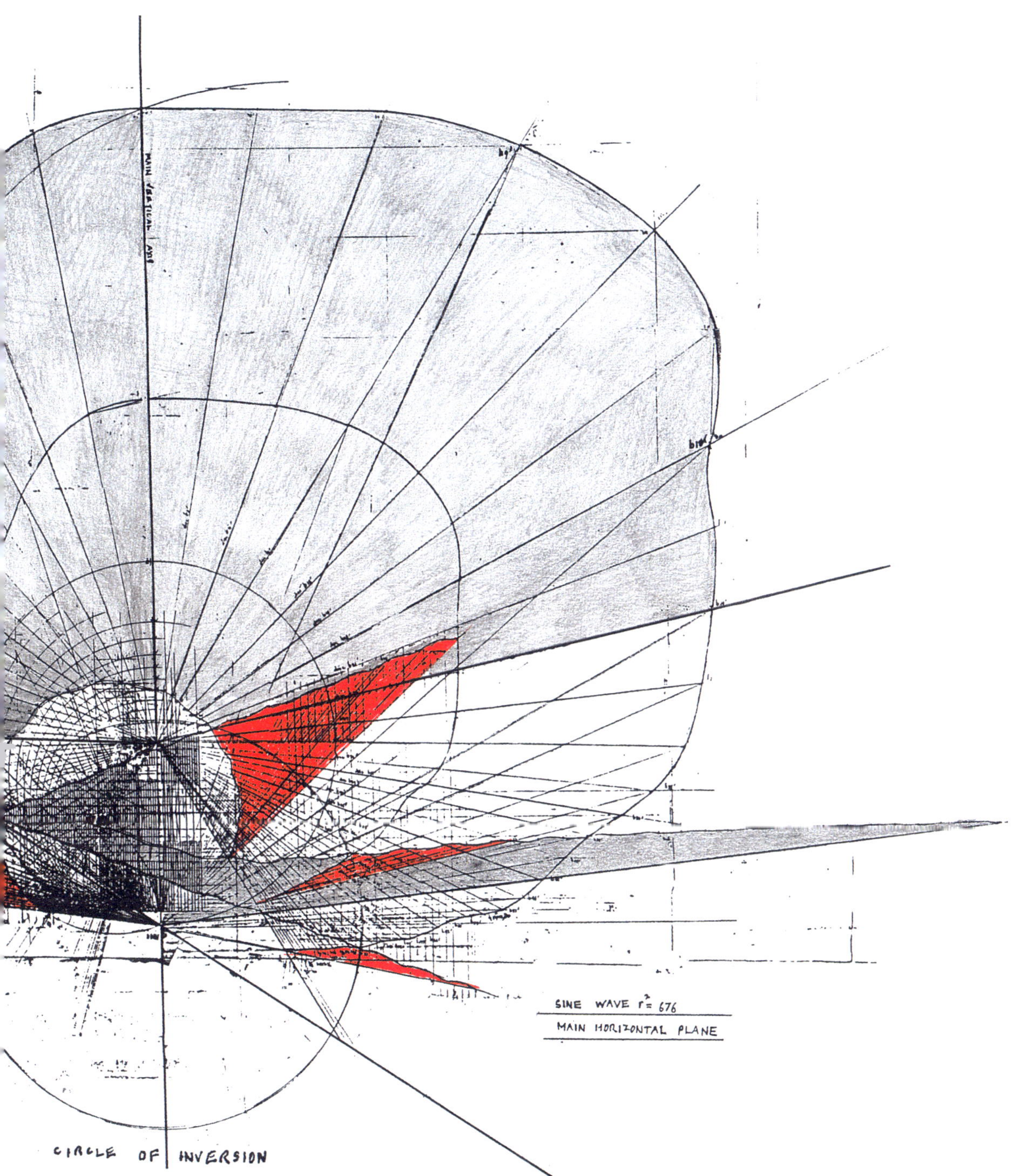

MAIN VERTICAL AXIS
bird
SINE WAVE r² = 676
MAIN HORIZONTAL PLANE
CIRCLE OF INVERSION

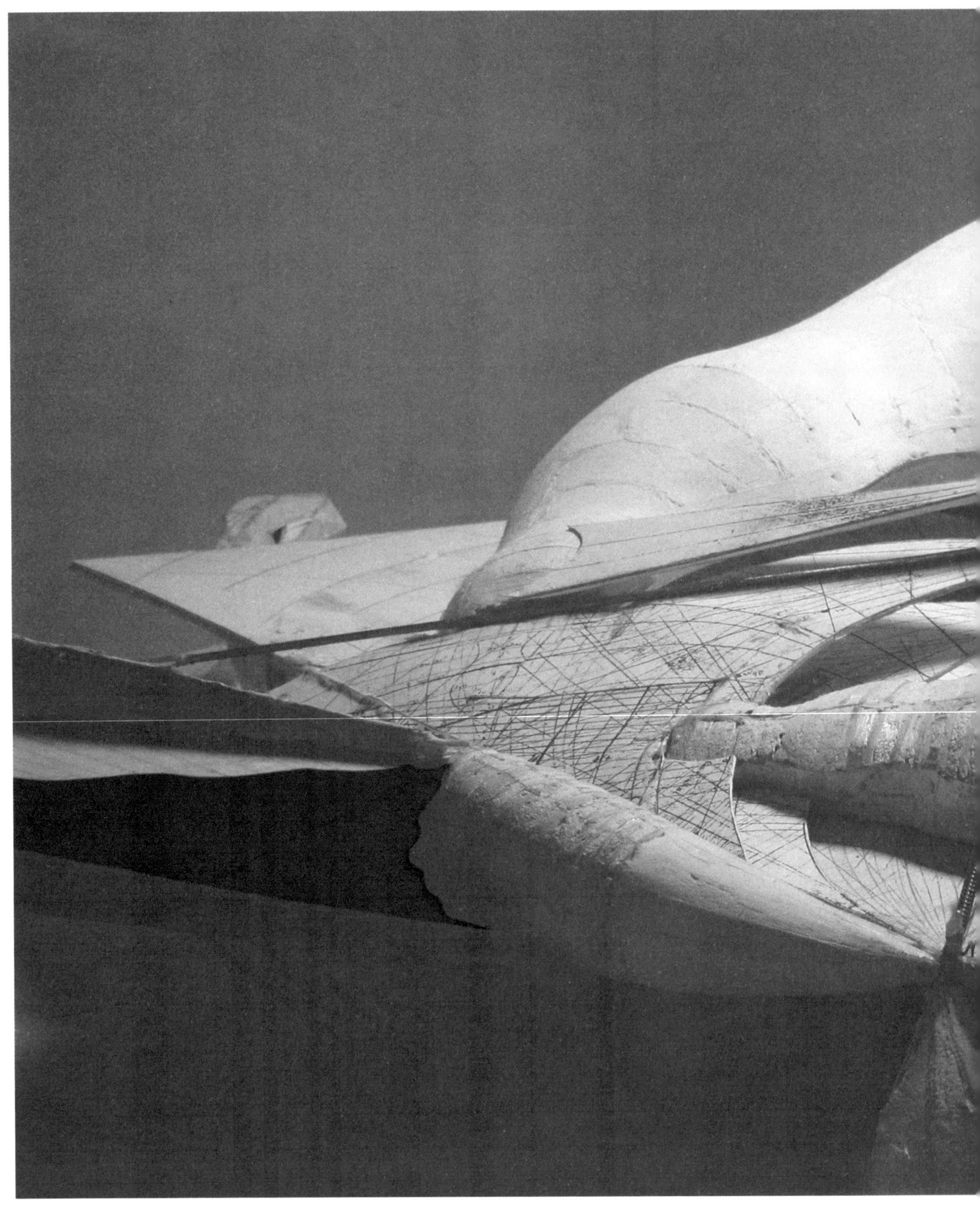

Inverting a corrugated cone with a sine wave profile with respect
to a point not lying on the cone or any part of the sine wave,
February 2003–October 2005. *Balsa wood, card, steel rods, wire
springs and cables.* 120 cm x 90 cm x 27 cm.

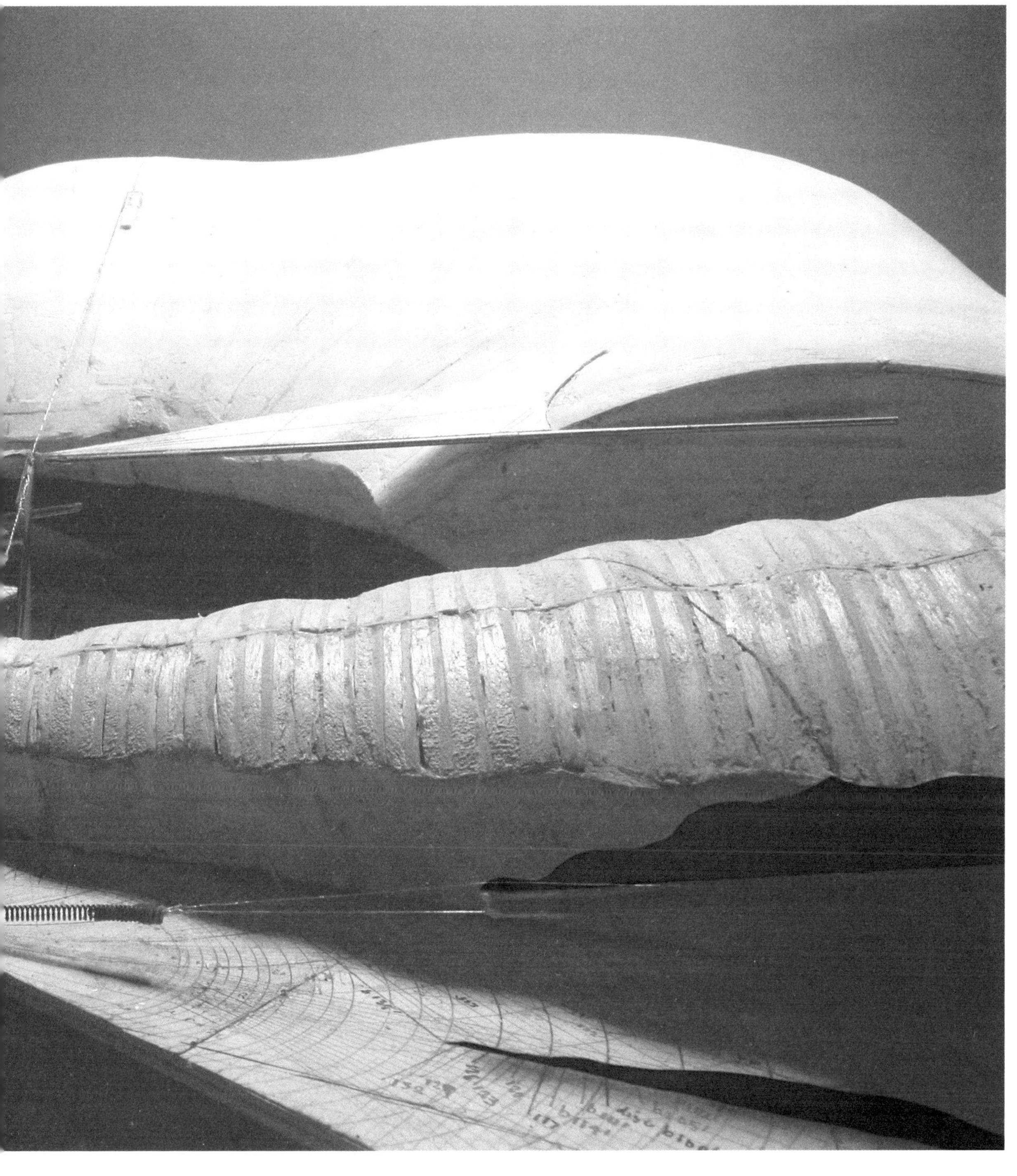

PERFECT IMPERFECT

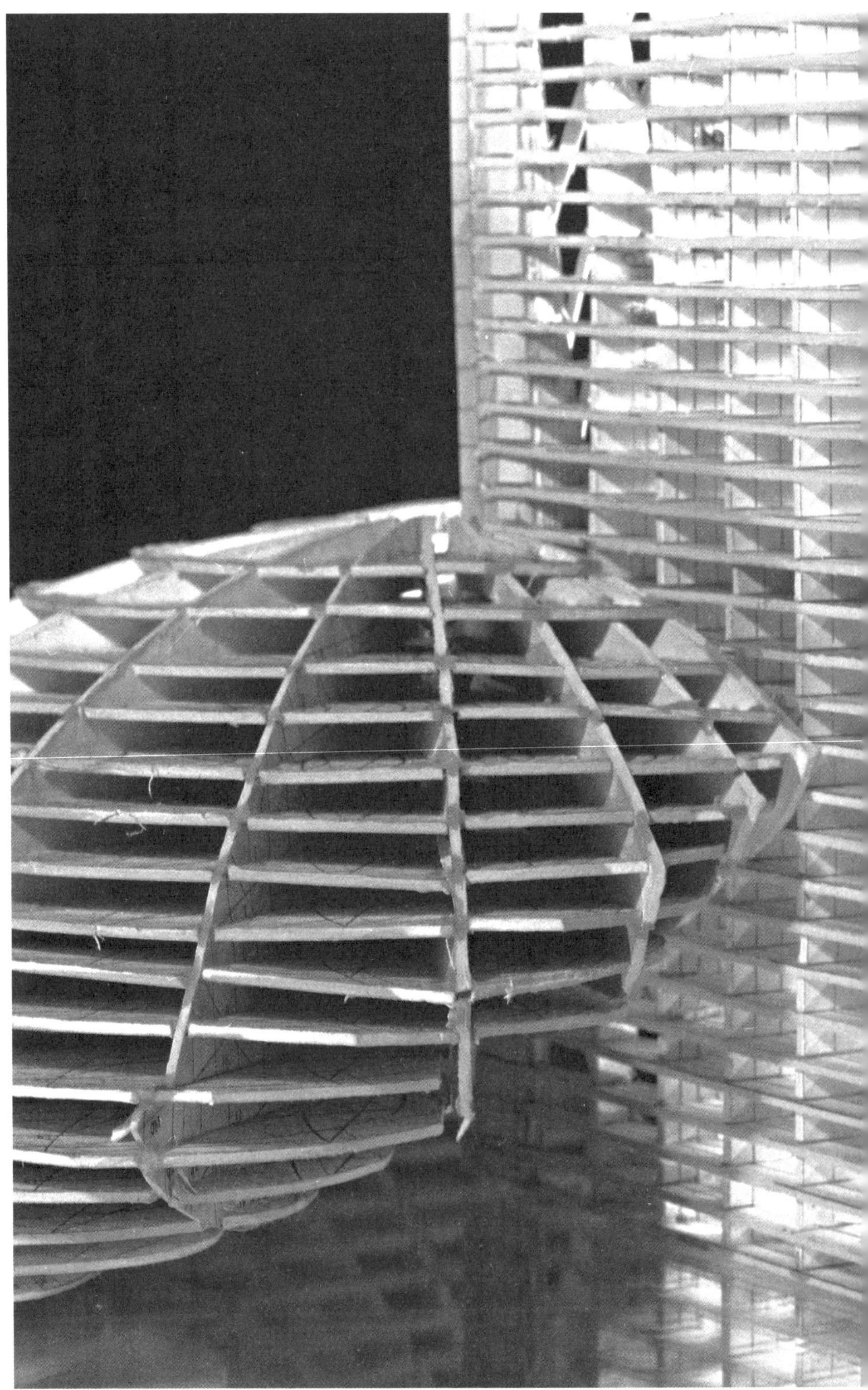

Inverting a cylinder CL
with respect to a point not
on the cylinder (detail).

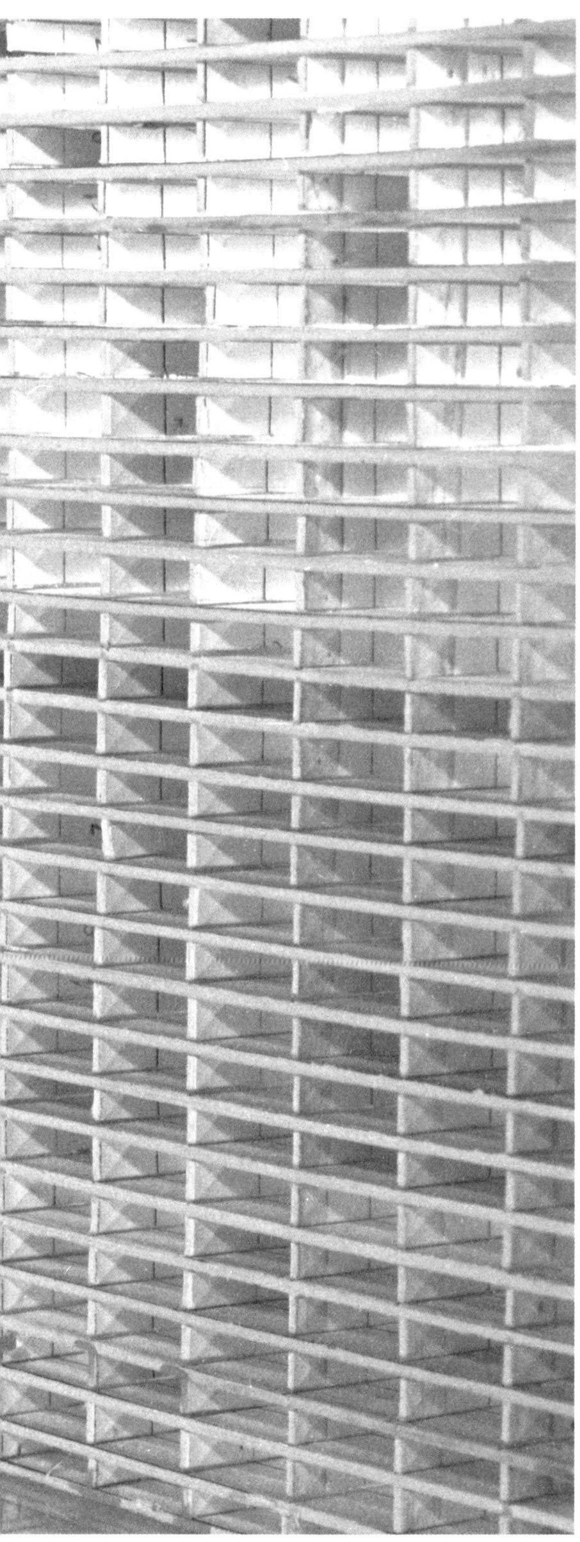

Perfect imperfect

MP . MQ = MR^2 – this is known as the inversion principle, and it is the basis of John Pickering's life-work. Using this rule, Pickering has defined an entire family of forms, and like all families, there is an air of inevitability about their appearance. Given the genetic base, the form has no choice but to come out in the wash: it is the totally predictable outcome of his chosen formula, generally expressed in cardboard, cut by hand from hand-calculated coordinates.

What does this strange algebra actually define? For a man who makes 3D objects, the choice of this 2D equation is odd. It means that before he can make anything Pickering has to map it onto the third dimension to give it mass, volume and shape. Only then can he, and we, consider the maths from outside, from any direction.

The equation itself defines an infinite number of possibilities, but it doesn't define all the world's possibilities (I guess this is the attraction). It generates either an infinite number of points, or a line, or perhaps the area bounded by the line. Yet when we look at his work it becomes clear that Pickering doesn't actually represent the equation directly but instead makes a jig on which to hold the answer. It is up to us, as observers, to construct the gossamer mathematical surface ourselves.

And from this observation flows the need for another layer of structure altogether: the framework to hold the envelope. On a practical level Pickering has to choose only a small proportion of all the possible points to use as the basis for his models. But in defining the rhythm of the supporting framework he has found that he has to give his objects a Corbusian language, separating the enclosure from the structure which defines and supports it. If you discuss this with him, he recognises it and his eyes twinkle as he says 'Well, I wondered if they could actually be used as architecture?'. Now there's a question. On a purely physical level, the answer has to be 'yes'. I've seen people living in worse places. Scaled up fifty-fold, these objects would have a logical structure, with a grid or a frame which could be made using conventional construction techniques. The pieces of card would become concrete walls and floors, the gaps in the surfaces could be filled by glass panels.

But as a basis for fledgling buildings, I feel Pickering's inversion principle is not really so good. The sheer obstinacy of the maths removes the possibility of adaptation, of flexibility, of the human bodging that is the hallmark of trial-and-error design. Mutation, good or bad, has no place in Pickering's world. Deliberate intervention does not feature either. There's no chance to 'add a bit here' if the volume ends up a bit mean or looks a bit wobbly: if one little piece is tweaked, everything else has to follow the inversion principle and change too, whether it wants to or not. Pickering's only way forward is backward: to start again on a new piece of work, painstaking step by painstaking step. Here lies the flaw in the approach, but also its richness.

At this point I think of Buddhist monks repeating the same mantra hour after hour, day after day, in an attempt to reach a state of grace. Like them, Pickering imposes an absolute discipline on himself. It is no accident that he chooses to take an unnecessarily tough route through his projects: everything is done laboriously by hand, modulating from one mathematical position to the next. It's as if he's playing his way through the piece, learning it as a musician. Pickering's interest in music reveals that he is in some way connecting maths and music, but once the parameters are defined, each mathematical 'note' becomes part of an inevitable sequence, built on its predecessor and itself defining the next note. The result is a little like the music boxes of old, not without charm nor sometimes great beauty.

Yet despite Pickering's best efforts, the physical manifestation of his carefully chosen maths is marvellously impure. As maths alone the answer has no impurities, but his way of working introduces imperfections into the pieces which gives them a certain humanity.

Why doesn't he take a shortcut and use modern technology to help him? John Pickering is a man who hasn't discovered Excel, or perhaps he has consciously refused the convenience of spreadsheet software with its ability to carry out the hundreds of calculations needed to define each of his forms. Instead, in an act of obstinacy bordering on self-sacrifice, he works through each repeat of the calculation by hand, hundreds of times, over and over again in a routine that you could say has become his life's fix, his drug. How comforting to Pickering must be the familiarity, the expectation, the inevitability of the flow of the numbers as they slowly unfold before him. Why else, if not addiction, would he work out dimensions to 1 mm in 10 km, ten thousand times the accuracy required to build these table-sized structures?

Perhaps there is an alternative explanation. The Pickering paradox lies in the gulf between the mathematical purity of the inversion principle and the physical imperfection of the work. Why build anything at all? Why not just leave the work as a string of pure numbers? Here I can only guess, but I imagine that for him there is much more to it than the numbers. I suspect that the importance of these pieces is private. Only he has experienced what's in there, and only he sees the sublime pathos as the mathematical language is gloriously revealed in its imprecise physical reality. Substance increasingly ceases to matter as long as the forms can simply exist as a framework onto which the pure numbers can be projected. So Pickering uses the shapes as the memory of his mathematical journey.

To return to his twinkle-eyed question, I don't believe Pickering's forms have a direct role as 'architecture'. One of the great things about humans is the way in which we adapt things to our purpose. Our whole world is full of physical lumps, bumps, holes and valleys that we carve into, build up, mine, chop down, blow up and reshape to suit ourselves. We do this with our artificial creations and buildings too. Yet Pickering's perfect imperfect forms are precise and inevitable, and cannot be changed. There is no question that they have a strength that comes from the rigour of the mathematical process involved in their conception, but at the same time they suffer from that rigour.

Pickering's work could certainly be built. As an engineer, I like the rationale of its manufacture,[1] but there is a fundamental contradiction in attempting to use his favourite equation for something like 'architecture'. This is because the inversion principle is the equation of a weightless structure. Put it on earth and the pure maths no longer applies. From this we can conclude that the proper place for Pickering's work is not on this earth, but in the weightlessness of space. This observation can also be levelled at the voguish architecture of mathematical idealisations with which Pickering's work might be compared. Put these mathematical forms on earth and another mathematical 'operator' – gravity – comes into play, pulling the lines of pure mathematical flux inevitably towards the ground. That's why we respond so well to arches, parabolas, catenaries and nets. The builders of the great cathedrals were fully aware of this, and designed their forms to respond to the flow. Pickering's work evokes shells, ripples and shockwaves that would be equally at home underwater, especially if they were made from something with a density of one tonne per cubic metre. Perhaps this explains the seabed-like language of the forms that spring from the maths. To live happily on the earth, Pickering's forms would be forced to thicken, shift, respond to and compromise the natural forces acting upon them.

Would I like to live in a Pickering creation? Only if you took away my backbone and turned me into jelly. Which is why I feel uncomfortable about the current fad for biomorphic forms, responding to a completely different set of drivers that may be familiar to echinoderms but not to homo sapiens. Yes they look great, and the spiral of a Nautilus shell has a poetry of its own, but that doesn't mean it's any better to live in than a box. In fact, for humans, it's worse, given that both our legs are the same length. Developing this theme takes us to an architectural language that has flat or nearly flat surfaces to walk on, but much more freedom in the rest of the enclosure. So the mathematical forms don't do it for me unless they are sheared through by great anarchic shards of floor, in which case there might be something mad and great to be found.

It's difficult to park in an empty carpark. In choosing the inversion principle as his very own parking space, John Pickering has put aside intuitive art and freedom of choice in favour of a 'highly liberating' precision. In his work he is partly an engineer – he changes the world to hold the product of his ideas. He is also a mathematician – and an ascetic. And he is a constructor of ideas whose mathematical purity can never be given physical form. How he copes with this dilemma I cannot imagine, but the remarkable thing is that he does. And he makes me want to know who's going to park in the next space. If I could choose who it would be, I would want someone to weld, graft, or mind-meld what Pickering does to those happily bashing out Tellytubby shapes in the name of architecture.

Chris Wise

[1]   It's a counterpoint to those who doodle away in 3D Studio without a second thought about the practicality of their computerised forms. They can draw whatever shape they like, but it either stays on a computer screen or something has to give somewhere. Either manufacturers develop techniques to enable these free forms to be built, or the 3D Studio jocks allow reality to constrain them. Personally, I hope the manufacturers rise to the challenge, and the advent of cadcam means that we are on the first steps of that journey. Not that John Pickering seems to worry too much about that: he is on a different journey.

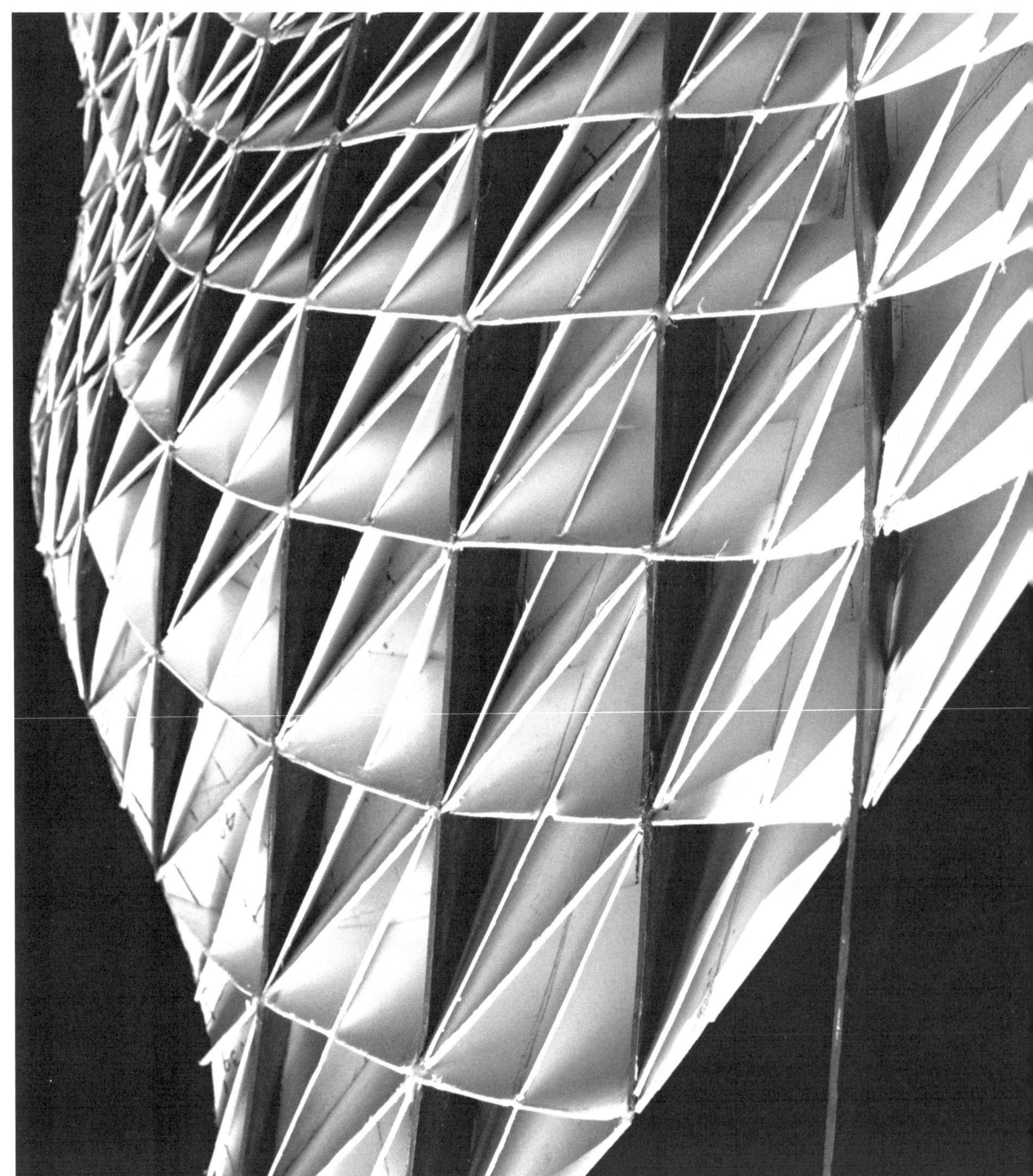

Inverting a sine wave with respect to a
point not lying on any part of the sine wave,
version 2, 2006 (detail of work in progress).
Card, plaster of Paris, steel rods,
58 cm x 47 cm x 34 cm.

Appreciation

John Pickering's work engages us at many levels. Its intriguing morphologies – the manifestation of complex geometry – invite us to explore surfaces as sculpture and to interpret volumes and spaces as architecture. Since we can read his work in all of these ways, we feel compelled to look at it more closely.

From a single fixed viewpoint, we attempt to explore the whole form, mentally rotating it. The gridded legibility of the surfaces and subtle patterns help us to understand and interpret the developed geometries. Then, as we physically move around these forms, we are surprised and delighted by unexpected interventions and developments of other complex forms. That delight is intensified by the realisation that these objects, though man-made, may evoke things found in nature, for example spiral seashells or the skeletal structures of sea sponges, plants and crystals. These are sculptures that appear to have 'grown', so their method of generation is evident from their form. The resulting dynamic is exciting because we engage the imagination in trying to understand the process, and project the form further or differently.

However, whilst John's work is exploratory, it is not accidental. He does not just plug some numbers into an equation and wait to see what happens. Instead, he has learned how to programme the equation to give birth to the end product that he imagines in his mind. In most cases, he says, he knows roughly what will happen, but there are always surprises, and occasionally those surprises cause him to start all over again.

When viewed out of context, these objects could be microscopically small or alternatively gigantic – or indeed any possible scale in between. So it is a vital part of their charm that we can interact with them at a human and tactile scale. In reality, however, because of the mathematical rigour involved, these fantastic creations are already potent, engineered, rational and, ultimately, buildable.

If ever conceived on a civic scale, John's sculptures would be incredible! In architecture we often devote a huge amount of effort to complex modelling in order to explore the origins of form – only to discover things in nature that show us the way. If the City Hall, the Reichstag Dome, the Air Museum at Duxford or the roof of the Great Court at the British Museum (all by Foster and Partners) are buildable as geometrically rationalised organic forms, then John's works are equally so.

In these sculptures the interaction of surface and volume, light and shadow, stimulate our visual senses, creating objects of contemplation. Furthermore, when photographed carefully, the models explode in scale; appearing in two dimensions, they have the impact of great constructivist paintings. Despite their fragile modelled form, these are fundamentally objects of immense power.

It would be quite fantastic to liberate John's work on a scale where everybody could interact with, explore and appreciate it. There are no intellectual boundaries here; this is natural, pure and empathetic sculpture for almost any environment. It attracts us because it feels right, and strangely familiar, yet it also has the power to intrigue, entertain and challenge our perceptions indefinitely.

John Silver

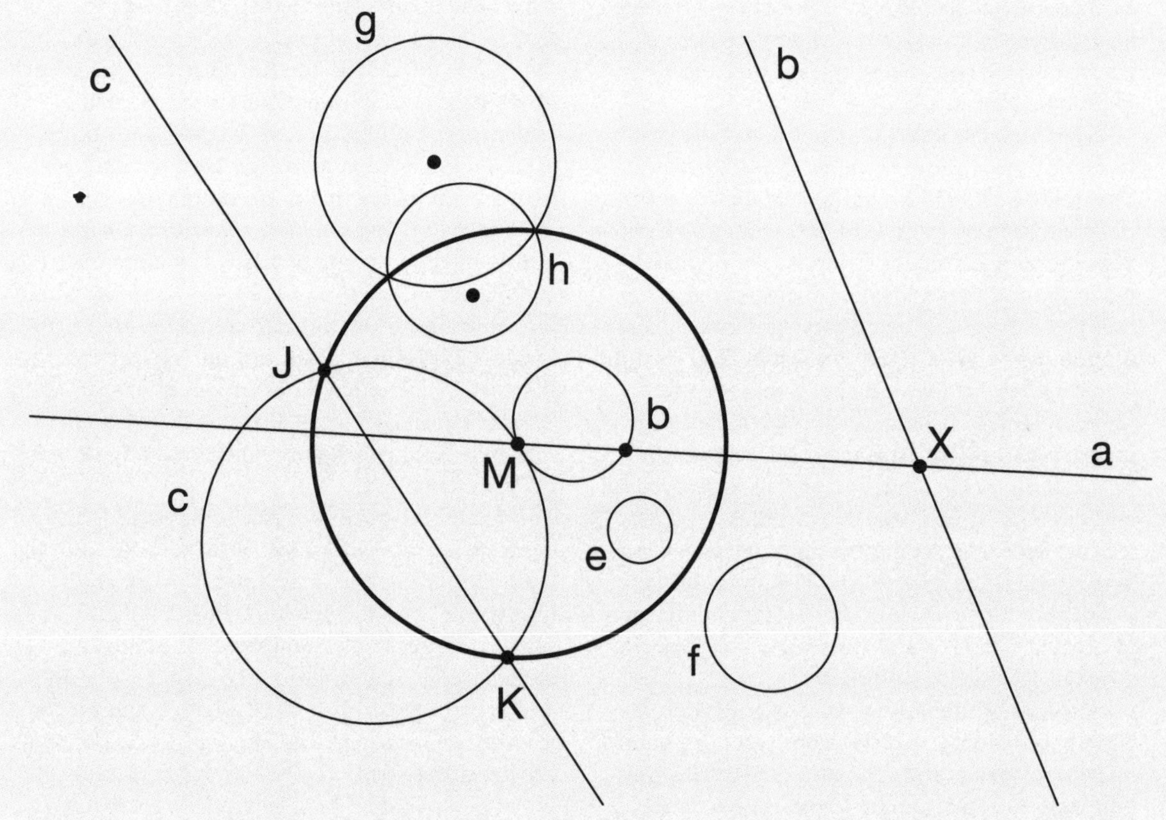

g
c
b
h
J
b
X
a
M
c
e
f
K

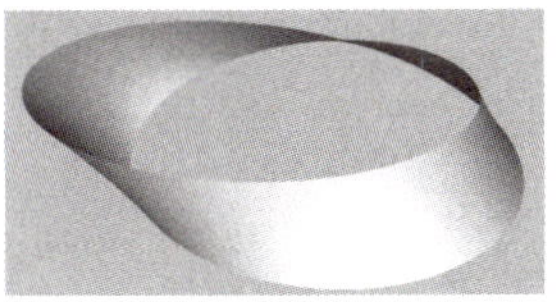

1

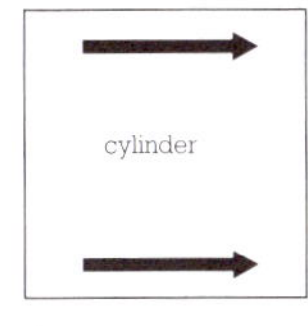

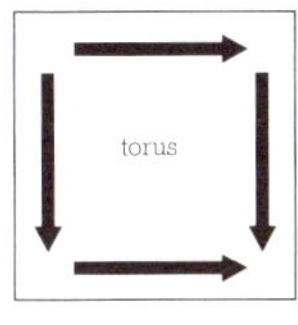

2

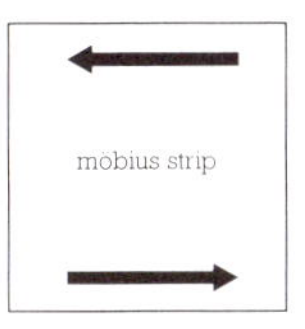

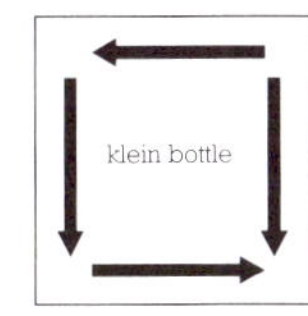

3

The geometry of inversion

Many artists use mathematics in their art and understand it intuitively, but they do not usually work directly with the concepts and extract new ideas from them in the way John Pickering does with the geometry of inversion. This essay brings together the ideas Pickering uses, but also includes some thoughts on the ways he wants to take his work further, particularly through the modern mathematics of fractals.

Topological models

Although much of John Pickering's work is centred on the transformation known as inversion, he was influenced at the outset by the models and concepts in Hilbert & Cohn-Vossen's *Geometry and the Imagination*. Among other things, this deals with the subject of topology.

Topology is sometimes called 'rubber sheet geometry' since it is concerned with properties like orientability, of which the classic example is the one-sided surface known as the Möbius strip or band, obtained by taking a strip of paper, giving it a twist and gluing the ends together. It has one edge and one surface.

(figure 1, Möbius strip)

It is a physical model which illustrates a conceptual idea. There are two other models that show more complex cases which John Pickering has created, the projective plane and the Klein bottle. All three, plus the cylinder and the torus, can be summarised by using a square which is stretched and joined in various ways. In each case the arrows must be joined to match; this may involve twisting which then gives a non-orientable surface.

(figure 2, joining a square to give a cylinder and torus)

The cylinder is commonly seen this way, by rolling up a square. If this cylinder is joined end to end with some compression, then the torus results. Pickering often uses the cylinder and the torus in his work, transforming them by inversion. The next pair are similar but contain one twist: the cylinder becomes a Möbius strip, while the torus becomes a Klein bottle with one straight join and one twist.

(figure 3, joining a square to give a Möbius strip and a Klein bottle)

Left: Principles of inversion, where M is the centre of the inverting circle.

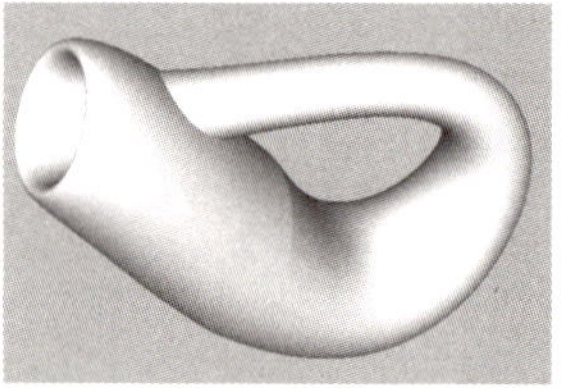
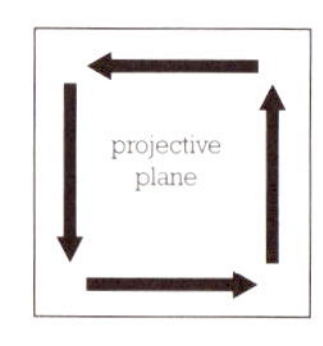

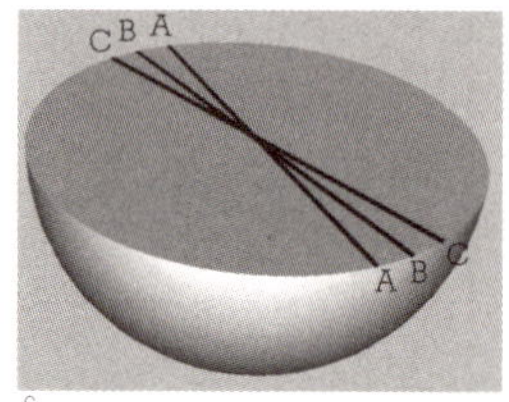

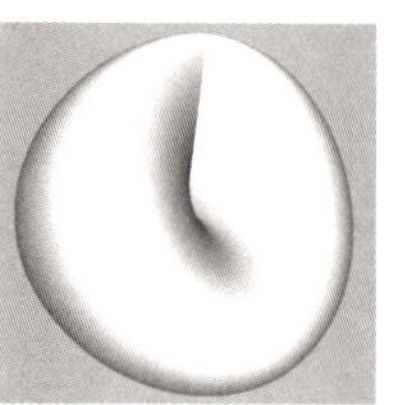
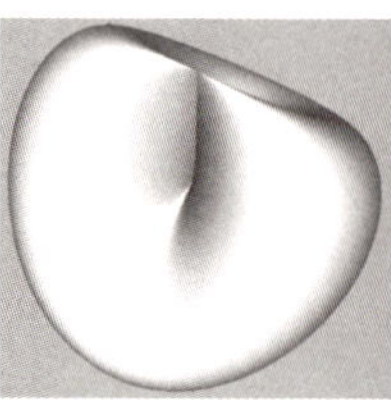

4   5   6   7

Because of the twist, it is not possible to model the Klein bottle in three-dimensional space without having it pass through itself.

(figure 4, Klein bottle)

The other possibility requires twisting when joining both edges and yields the projective plane.

(figure 5, joining a square for a projective plane)

The projective plane is used everyday by artists who project space onto a two-dimensional canvas. Geometrically (rather than topologically) it consists of the Euclidean plane where every pair of parallel lines meet in a single line, the line at infinity, which is the artist's horizon line. Projective geometry has a link to Pickering's work on inversion, but he also produced a sculpture of the projective plane which is shown on page 41. The square gives too crude a result, so the hemisphere is used instead. Points must be joined as in figure 6.

(figure 6, joining a hemisphere to give a projective plane)

This joining of the same lettered points is achieved by using a 'cap'. The special cap relies on the property that a projective plane with a hole is a Möbius strip. This is brought together so that it crosses itself (much in the same way as the Klein bottle must interpenetrate) and so is known as a cross-cap and resulting surface, shown as two views in figure 7.

(figure 7, cross-cap surface)

This is easy to do on the computer, but harder to make physically due to the crossing. Pickering's interpretation is shown on page 41.

If you slice through the top of the cross-cap, you get a curve called a lemniscate. This curve has interested John Pickering since he came across it in conjunction with inversion.

(figure 8, sliced cross-cap)

The concept and history of inversion

In the first few decades of the nineteenth century there was a revolution in the field of mathematics as the standard geometry of Euclid was replaced by more pliable systems. The question of non-Euclidean geometry (where parallel lines meet more than once) was tackled independently by János Bolyai, Carl Frederick Gauss and Nicolas Lobachevsky. Bolyai wrote in 1823:

> *I have discovered things so wonderful*
> *that I was astounded … Out of nothing*
> *I created a whole new world.*

This sentiment could equally well apply to the worlds created by another type of geometry, that of the inversive plane, which was discovered around the same time. Just as non-Euclidean geometry was discovered independently, so too was inversion, but in a less clear fashion. The two geometries are related, in that inversion was used by Henri Poincaré at the end of the century as a tool to model hyperbolic geometry, familiar to most in the circular tilings of Escher. Both geometries are mappings, but their results differ widely.

There is some debate about who discovered inversion and stereographic projection, but it seems to have been explored almost simultaneously in the 1820s, in Belgium by Adolphe Quetelet and Germinal Dandelin, in Germany by Jacob Steiner and Heinrich Gustav Magnus, and in France by Jean-Victor Poncelet. It was used in many different ways to solve a variety of problems before it settled down as a concept. By the 1840s, however, Stubbs and Ingram in Ireland were writing papers on the transformation of

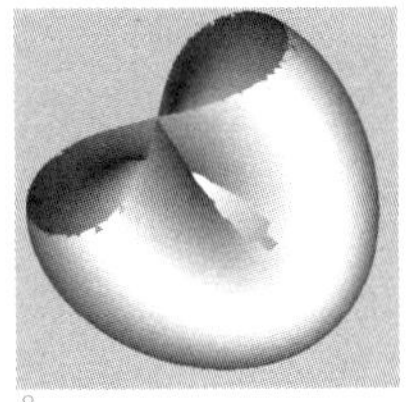

8

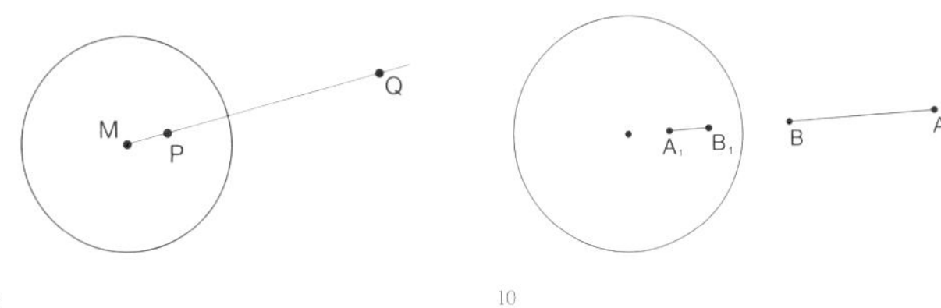

9

10

curves, treated in the way I describe below. Another reason inversion is difficult to pin down is that it can be invoked in an almost trivial way to prove theorems or achieve constructions that otherwise are extremely difficult to carry out. With respect to Pickering's work, once you know the 'secret' behind it, the stunning results are easy to understand, and they are further enhanced by the knowledge of this gem of geometry.

Inversion basics

Inversion is simple. In the plane it is a kind of reflection in a circle, which maps all points inside a circle to points outside and vice versa; with the centre of the circle being a special point where all points at infinity map. In space, the mapping is of the inside and outside of a sphere.

(figure 9, inversion)

In figure 9, point P inside the circle is mapped to point Q. The distances of the points from the centre are related by the formula:

$$MP \cdot MQ = r^2 \text{ where } r \text{ is the radius of the circle.}$$

The term *inversion* arises because, to find the length MQ in order to find the inverse point to point P, the formula is rearranged so that

$$MQ = \frac{r^2}{MP}$$

The same formula applies when using a sphere, with r as the radius of the sphere. In both cases it is necessary to draw the line to the point being inverted in space, measure the length and then calculate the length to the inverse point, knowing the radius of the

inverting circle or sphere. John Pickering uses a hand calculator to invert points. Knowing how inversion affects lines and circles and other curves, he does not calculate every point. The concept of inversion also applies when you consider inverting objects.

(figure 10, reflection in a circle = inversion)

The direction of the segment AB is inverted in its reflection in the circle so whereas A is furthest from the centre, A_1 is now closest. Since the segment AB is on a line through the centre of the circle, it remains a line segment. The length has also altered, which would not happen if reflecting in a line or plane. This has consequences if you are constructing a sequence of points. For example, if you spaced them equally on segment AB, they would no longer be equal on segment A_1B_1.

Figure 11 (shown on the opening page of this essay and overleaf) sums up the following properties of inversion (where M is the centre of the inverting circle):

·   Straight lines through the centre of inversion are self-inverse, i.e. line a inverts to line a, although the corresponding points are different

·   Straight lines not passing through the centre of inversion invert to circles passing through the centre of inversion: lines b and c invert to circles b and c

·   A point on the inverting circle inverts to the same point, eg. points J and K

·   Lines which intersect the inverting circle

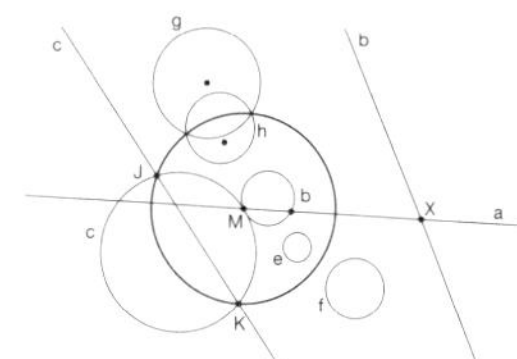 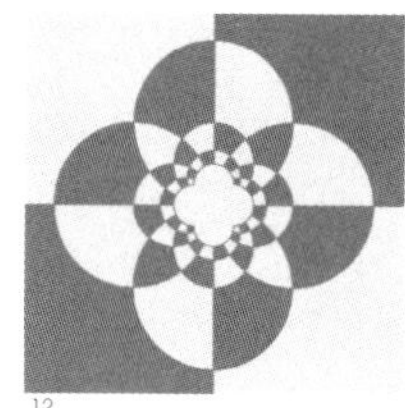 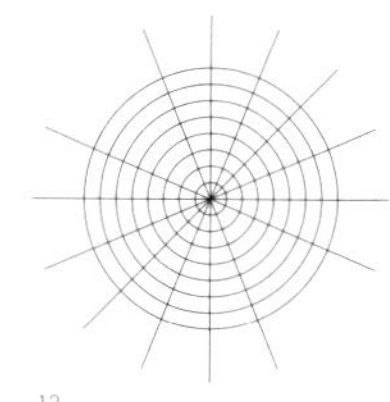 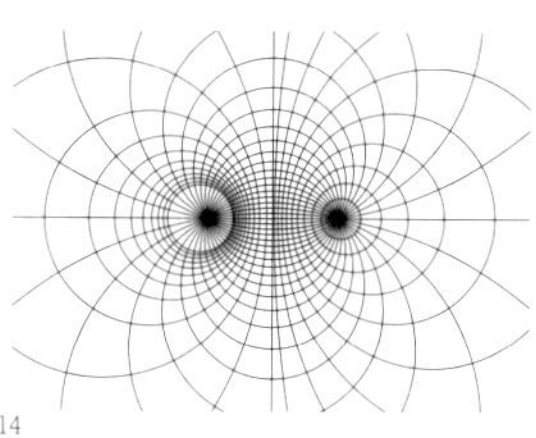

invert to circles intersecting the inverting circle at the same points, eg. points J and K

· Circles always invert to circles; circle e inverts to f and vice versa, similarly g and h

· Circles that pass through the centre invert to straight lines; circle b inverts to line b

· When a circle is inverted, its centre does not invert to the centre of the new circle, eg. with circles g and h; this is important and is discussed below

· When two entities which intersect are inverted, the points of intersection invert to the intersection points of their corresponding inverted entities; point X, the intersection of lines a and b inverts to the intersection of circle b and line a

· Inversion is 'reversible': when a point that has been inverted is also inverted with respect to the same circle, it returns to the original point; this is also known as an involution

· Inversion is conformal; this means that angles are preserved, although inverted (this is discussed below).

· All points on the line at infinity (in perspective terms the horizon) are inverted into the centre of the circle

There are two classic diagrams that I think reflect the striking visual results possible with inversion, particularly as Pickering has developed it in three dimensions. The first, an early piece of mathematical Op art, was created by the mathematician Herman von Baravalle who was prominent in the Waldorf schools in the USA. It is the inversion of a chequerboard. The full chequerboard extends quite a way out. The inverting circle is tangent to the four larger circular arcs which are shown sitting within the four central squares. The four internal circular arcs are the inverse of the outer sides of the chequerboard.

(figure 12, inversion of a chequerboard)

The next diagram shows the inversion of a set of concentric circles with a set of lines through their centres:

(figure 13, polar grid)

The inverting circle is chosen on one of the intersections of the lines and circles and gives the result shown in figure 14. The inversion gives two sets of circles, one from the concentric circles and one from the lines. The inverting circle is centred on the left limiting point and has a radius equal to the distance between the two centres. Each of the circles that do not meet is the inverse of one of the concentric circles. They include as limiting cases the two points inside the smallest circle and the vertical line of symmetry, which can be thought of as a circle of infinite diameter. Those with a centre falling outside the inverting circle give rise to the circles on the left, and so have a different spacing from those on the right. Every circle in the other set of circles passes through the two limiting points of the first set, and includes the horizontal axis of symmetry as a special case. It has two 'imaginary' limiting points. (Note: imaginary

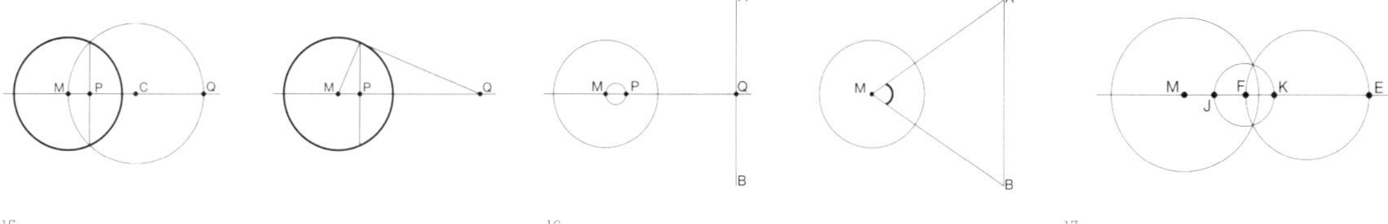

15 16 17

points are discussed on page 94.) Since inversion is a conformal transformation, and the radial lines are orthogonal – crossing at right angles – this also means that every circle of the first set crosses every circle of the second set orthogonally.

(figure 14, inversion of a polar grid)

Geometrical constructions

There are many geometrical constructions for finding an inverse point and they usually come in pairs to accommodate the initial point inside or outside the circle. This is one such pair.

(figure 15, construction of inverse points)

In both cases, a point is being inverted in the circle centre M. Since inversion is reversible, P is the inverse of Q and Q is also the inverse of P. The construction at the left is for inverting point Q, which is outside the circle; the one at the right is for inverting point P, which is inside. To invert point Q outside, bisect the segment MQ between Q and the centre of the inverting circle at C and draw a circle radius CQ. Join the points where this circle cuts the inverting circle and intersect MQ at the inverse point P. For the point P inside, join P to the centre of the inverting circle, M. Draw a perpendicular to this line to intersect the inverting circle and then join this intersection to M. Draw a perpendicular to this line so that it cuts the line MP at Q.

When constructing inversions of lines and circles, the work is simplified by taking note of the properties of inversion described above. John Pickering's skill has been to analyse the objects he has been working with so that he can minimise the amount of calculation. For example, suppose you want to invert the line segment AB in figure 16. Drop the perpendicular from

M, the centre of the inverting circle, to give point Q. Join Q to the centre of the inverting circle. Invert to point P. Knowing that the line inverts to a circle through the centre, then MP is the diameter of the circle and bisecting MP gives its centre. Join M to A and B and intersect the circle which is the inverse of AB. This gives the arc which is the inverse of the segment AB.

(figure 16, inversion of an arc)

The inverse of a circle is a circle, so you only need to find the inverse of two points at the end of a diameter. In figure 17, M is the centre of the inverting circle. Draw a line through M, the centre of the inverting circle, to intersect the circle being inverted at E and F. Invert these points to give J and K respectively. The centre of the inverted circle is then halfway between J and K. As a check, note that the circle being inverted intersects the inverting circle, so the inverted circle must go through these points of intersection.

(figure 17, calculation diagram for circle inversion)

Pickering uses diagrams like these when he works with objects in space. He finds suitable intersecting planes.

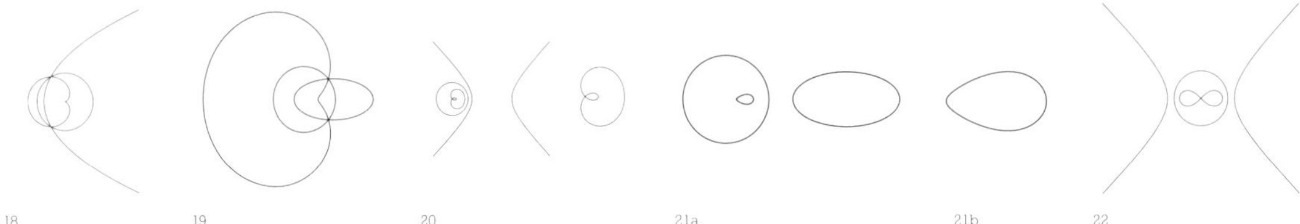

	first curve	centre of inversion as point of first curve	centre of inversion as point of second curve	second curve
1	Parabola	focus	cusp point	cardioid
2	Ellipse or hyperbola	focus	pole or node	limaçon
3	Rectangular hyperbola	centre	centre	lemniscate
4	Ellipse	not on focus		oval
5	Archimedean spiral	point not on pole	inflexion point	double spiral

Two-dimensional inversion of curves

John Pickering was influenced by E. H. Lockwood's *A Book of Curves* (1961), which contains many practical ways to draw curves and has many references to inversion. The following are some examples, inspired by the book, to illustrate the properties of inversion. Inversion of all curves, apart from a circle and a line, yields different resulting curves depending on the position of the centre of inversion, so some positions are for showing the inversive relationship of well-known curves. Since inverting is an involution, repeating the inversion on the second curve takes you back to the first one, so there are two inversion centres given in the table above where the centre is a significant point of the second curve. These curves are shown in the following diagrams, which all show the position of the inverting circle.

(figure 18, inversion of parabola/cardioid)

The cardioid (heart-shaped) curve is the inversion of the complete parabola. Its cusp corresponds to the point where the parabola touches the line at infinity. The cardioid is one of a family of curves called limaçons (referring to their snail shape).

Since the conics can all be considered as projec-

tions of a circle, then the different conics all invert to one of the limaçon family if the centre of inversion is the focus of the conic. For an ellipse, the limaçon has a rounded node in contrast to the cusp of the cardioid.

(figure 19, inversion of ellipse/limaçon)

The hyperbola inverts into a limaçon which crosses itself. This models the way the hyperbola intersects the line at infinity. Figure 20 shows the inversion of the hyperbola/limaçon.

(figure 20, inversion of hyperbola/limaçon)

If the centre of inversion is not the focus of a conic, then different curves result. So the ellipse inverts to an egg shape at one point. Figure 21 illustrates how the inverse mapping gives a small egg, so it is magnified at the right.

(figure 21a, inversion of ellipse; 21b, enlarged result)

If the hyperbola is a rectangular hyperbola (where the asymptotes are perpendicular) and the centre of inversion is the centre of the hyperbola, it inverts into a lemniscate (bow-shaped curve).

(figure 22, inversion of rectangular hyperbola/lemniscate)

This result can be used to illustrate another property of the lemniscate. If you invert all the lines of a hyperbola drawn by means of tangents using the

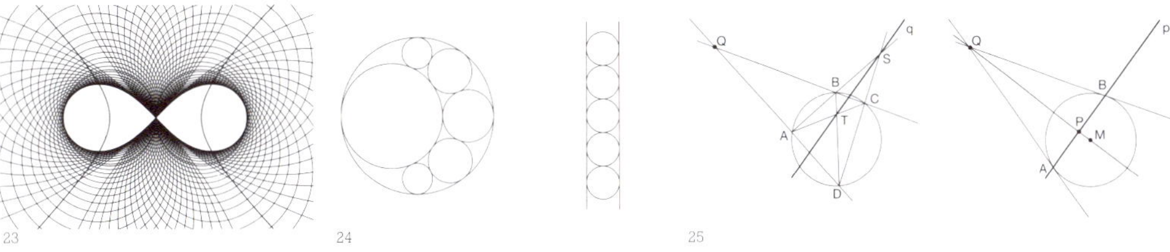

centre as centre of inversion, then the lines invert into circles which form the envelope of a lemniscate. This diagram also illustrates the property of inversion whereby it is the position of the centre, rather than the radius, that is important for defining the shape of the inverted curve. The radius defines the size, so that figure 23 has a larger radius for the circle of inversion, though the lemniscate is the same shape as in the previous one.

(figure 23, lemniscate as envelope of circles)

An example of working with inversion
The above examples of inversion of curves show one of the powerful transformation aspects of inversion, but it really comes into its own when you consider inverting circles and lines. For example, drawing the figure on the left of figure 24 is not easy, but if you think of it as the diagram on the right and invert it, then it becomes trivial. This kind of insight is essential for cutting down the amount of work involved, especially if, like Pickering, you calculate by hand.

(figure 24, inversion of circles between two lines)

Knowing the properties of inversion also tells you that the centre of the inverting circle is where the two outer circles of the ring touch. This follows from the property that the inverse of a line always gives a circle through the centre of inversion.

Links between inversion and perspective and more
Figure 12 is a good example of how the spacing of lines changes when the lines are inverted, becoming closer together the nearer they get to the centre of the inverting circle. This spacing is related to the way the lines get closer together in a perspective drawing of a grid, known as foreshortening. This is not surprising since the inversive mapping takes all points at infinity to the centre, whereas in perspective all points at infinity in a plane map onto the horizon line. There is another indirect link to Pickering's interests here, that of music. Mathematically, the inversion of a number gives its harmonic, so $\frac{1}{2}$ is the harmonic of 2 and musicians refer to harmonic intervals in terms such as fourths and fifths. This should not be confused with musical inversion which is a reflection. The spacing that occurs in both inversion and perspective foreshortening is also seen more obviously in the frets of a guitar which can be constructed in the same way for a Pythagorean tuning (but not equal temperament). Perspective gave rise to projective geometry, which describes transformations in the projective plane. One of its fundamental axioms is that of duality, where lines and points can be exchanged in theorems. By chance, it is possible to construct dual diagrams through the concept of pole and polar in a conic. One way to do this is shown in figure 25, which is illustrated as a circle, although it could be applied to any conic.

(figure 25, pole and polar construction to inverse point)

To construct the polar line (bold line q) of the point Q with respect to the conic, first draw any two lines through Q to cut the conic at A, B, C and D. Join AB and DC and intersect at S. Join AC and BD to intersect

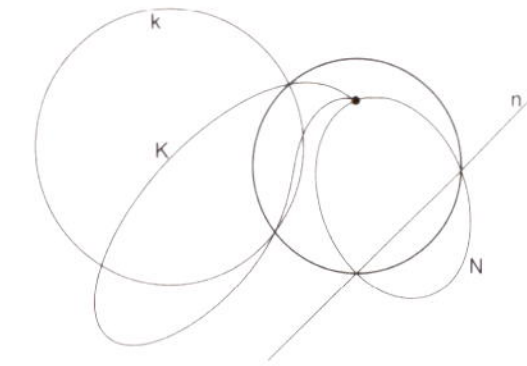

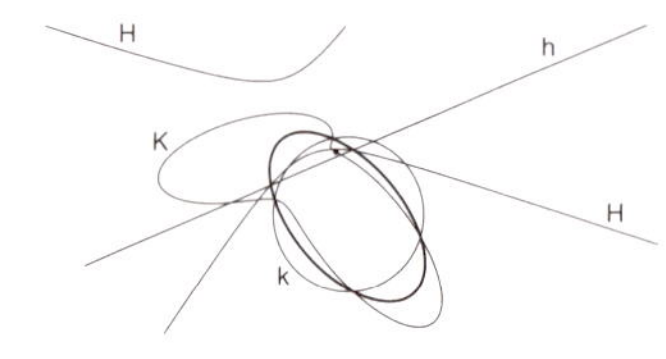

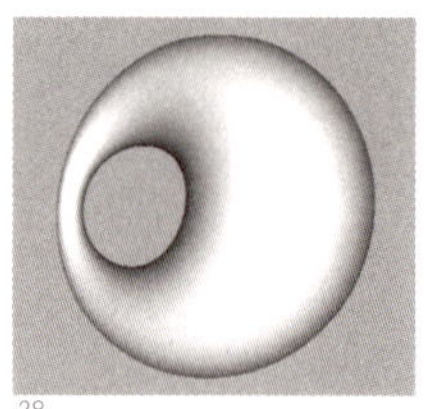

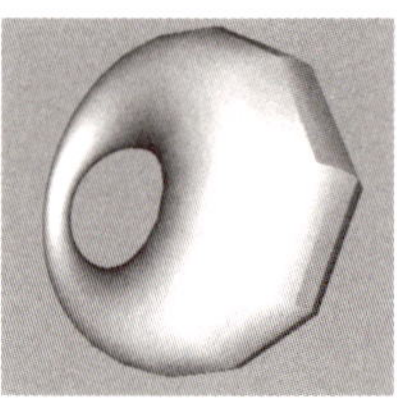

26

27

28

at T. Then ST is the polar line (q). There is not space to go into detail about how this is connected to perspective, other than to say that if the line QS is drawn as the horizon line then ABCD is the perspective image of a square with Q and S the vanishing points.

If the centre of the circle (M) is joined to Q, then the point of intersection with the polar line q and the pole point Q gives P, which is the inverse of Q (as in the right of figure 25). Since the pole and polar construction only require a ruler, this gives another simple construction. Now, if points A and D move towards one another (and similarly with B and C), they will at some position coincide and QD will be a tangent to the circle. This is the same construction as in figure 15.

The purpose of this construction is also to show that inversion is a special case of a general transformation known as a quadratic transformation. Taking any point of the plane as a centre of the transformation C and any conic, the transformation of any point of the plane P to its conjugate point is achieved by constructing the polar line of P, joining P to the centre C and intersecting them. This opens up a huge set of possibilities that requires a computer to realise. The results are more complex since they are not circle-preserving transformations. Figures 26 and 27 show some examples.

(figure 26, quadratic transformation using a circle)

In figure 26, a line (n) and a circle (k) have been transformed with the conic becoming a circle. The line becomes an ellipse (N) and the circle a tear-drop-shaped curve with a cusp (K). The centre can be seen where the tip of the cusp meets the ellipse.

(figure 27, quadratic transformation using an ellipse)

In figure 27, a line (h) and a circle (k) have been transformed with the conic an ellipse. The line becomes a hyperbola (H) and the circle a doubly indented curve. The centre can be seen where the two curves intersect.

This transformation is too varied to illustrate, and the curves change very markedly as the relative positions of the defining elements change. Thus it is harder to visualise, and can only be calculated with a computer implementation which uses dynamic geometry. The procedure can be extended to three dimensions as shown by the examples in figures 29 and 30.

Inversion in three dimensions

To study inversion in space – as John Pickering does – a sphere is used instead of a circle. The principles can be summarised as follows:

·   All properties that apply to plane inversion also apply to inversion in a sphere

·   Planes through the centre of inversion are self-inverse

·   Planes not through the centre of inversion invert to spheres through the centre of inversion

·   A circular disk inverts so that the planar portion becomes part of the surface of a sphere (a cap) bounded by the inverted circle

·   A point on the inverting sphere inverts to the same point

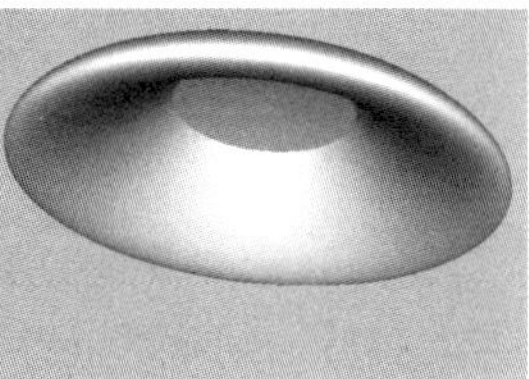
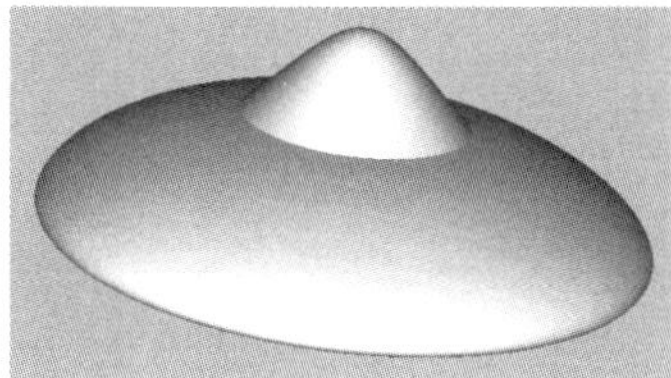
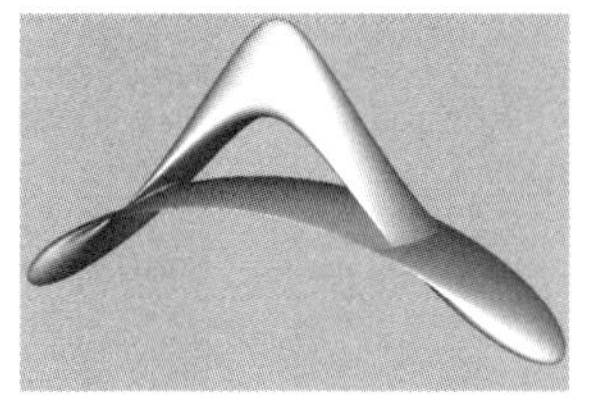
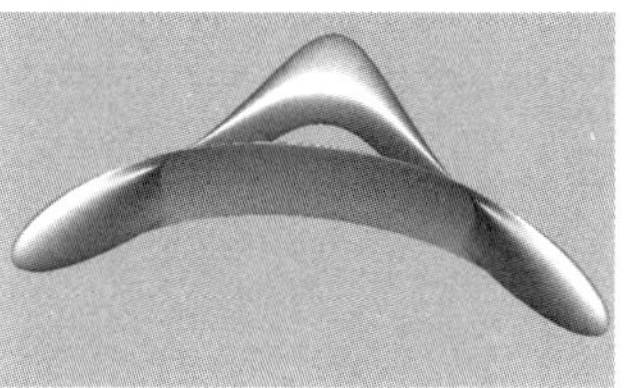

29

30

· Spheres not through the centre always invert
to spheres

· Spheres which pass through the centre
invert to planes

· When a sphere is inverted, the centre of
the sphere does not invert to the centre of
the new sphere (similarly for the other
properties, like conformality, described
above in the plane)

· Since a plane section of a sphere is a circle, figure
9 and the formula $MP \cdot MQ = r^2$ applies equally
well in space as it does in the plane.

It is very easy to study inversion in the plane, even
without a computer, but three dimensions is a different matter. Because circles and spheres invert into
themselves, what has been studied is the inversion of
surfaces that can be constructed from them. The torus
is the widest class formed from envelopes of spheres
whose centres lie on a curve which is a subset of
these surfaces. A torus is generated by taking a circle
in a plane, choosing a line in the plane to act as axis
and sweeping the circle around the axis. The axis may
be outside the circle, in which case the familiar torus
ring (a bagel shape) is obtained, but it can also intersect the circle or be tangent to it, in which case it
gives rise to a horn and a spindle torus respectively.

Because of the way inversion brings all points at
infinity to the centre, the inversion of the cone, the
cylinder and the torus gives rise to similar entities
which are called cyclides. Cyclides are important in
computer graphics as patches for joining surfaces.

The photographs of the so-called Dupin cyclides in
Hilbert and Cohn-Vossen's book, *Geometry and the
Imagination*, are evident in much of Pickering's work.
Dupin cyclides have the property that all their lines of
curvature are circles and that they are always the
inversion of a torus. Pickering has been able to identi-
fy the circles in the torus and invert them to a circle, a
fact which simplified his work, but also gave him an
advantage over someone who works with a computer
and merely calculates points. If you work from a mesh,
you need to take care that the mesh is dense enough.
Otherwise, because inversion is an uneven transform,
you will get angular surfaces. Figure 28 shows the
same Dupin cyclide calculated from a low- and high-
density mesh torus.

(figure 28, cyclide from inversion of a torus with different mesh density)

These artefacts could be exploited if you wanted
angular faces and not smooth ones, as commonly
occurs with triangulation in computer-designed
architecture. Pickering also works in planes so that
where he only uses part of a cyclide, he obtains what
looks like part of a stadium. So his studies of three-
dimensional inversion are a small fraction of the
possibilities. There is even more to explore with
quadratic transformations. Figures 29 and 30 are two
examples using a sphere as the transforming conic.

(figure 29, two views of a quadratic transformation of a sphere)

(figure 30, two views of a quadratic transformation of a torus)

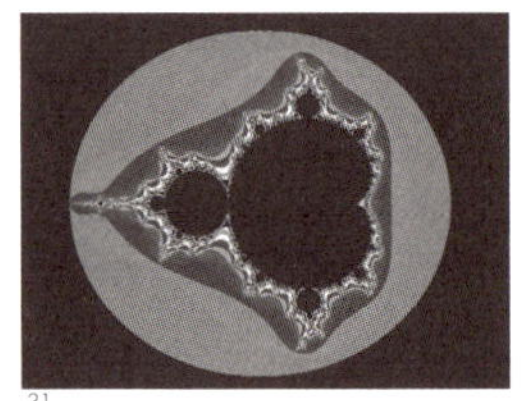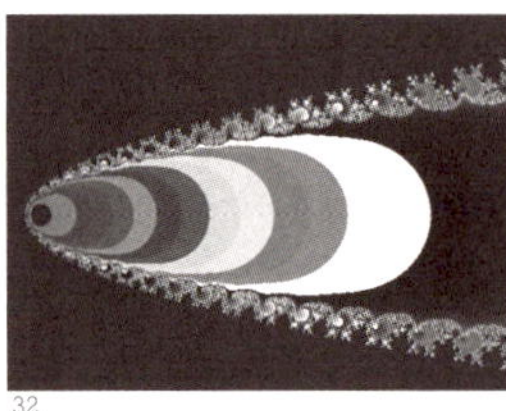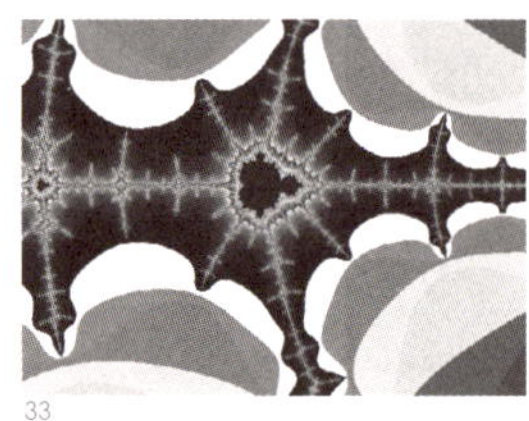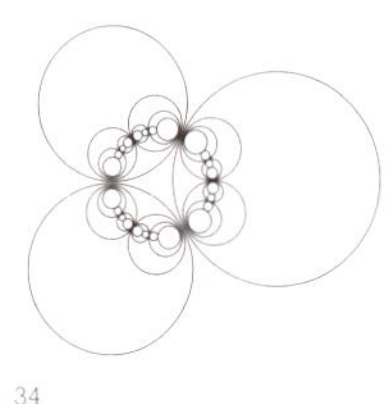

John Pickering has been working with an area of geometry which is very fertile, but he knows there are other aspects to explore. The following ideas give an indication of some of these.

Geometry and the imaginary and the complex plane

One of Pickering's inspirations, Hilbert and Cohn Vossen's *Geometry and the Imagination*, contains a small section on a wider aspect of geometry concerning numbers called complex numbers and the complex plane involving the square root of minus 1, which is given the symbol i (although engineers frequently use j). A complex number is symbolised as z, where $z = a + bi$. There is not room to go into detail here, but it has one important direct relationship to inversion which often causes confusion: it is possible to invert in a circle with radius i.

Remembering that the inverse of point P to point Q obeys the formula that $MP \cdot MQ = r^2$, where r is the radius of the circle, then if this radius is i (with the centre in a real point), its square becomes -1 and the inversion reflects the point through the centre of the inverting circle. This is sometimes called point inversion. The effect on a curve is a rotation through the centre by 180°. In modern mathematics, inversion is seen as a small part of a set of transformations in the complex plane which are conformal (preserve angles) but which may or may not preserve circles. (Anyone wanting to follow John Pickering's lead will find rich pickings there too.)

The Mandelbrot set and other fractals

The Mandelbrot set is possibly the most famous case where non-mathematicians have come across the complex plane. It is the result of investigating the points of the complex plane using the complex function $z^2 + c$, where the constant c is also a complex number. You apply the function iteratively; that is, you continually feed the result of your calculation back into the function. In the classic Mandelbrot set, c is the point of the complex plane. You find that when you perform the calculation, the result is either attracted to a fixed point or to infinity. The black-and-white version indicates points which fall into one of these classes, the Mandelbrot set being the set of numbers which do not tend to infinity. Coloured images measure the speed at which the iteration goes to infinity. Inversion is inherent in its study, but I have never seen the following curiosity illustrated.

(figure 31, Mandelbrot set)

Turned on its side, the main body of the Mandelbrot set is often called the 'gingerbread man' with a cardioid body. If you invert it (at the cusp) you get a parabolic shape, as with the pure curves shown in figure 18.

(figure 32, inversion of Mandelbrot set)

If you zoom in close to the left edge, the gingerbread man appears many times. Remarkably, although the image has been transformed by inversion, the self-similarity is preserved. It is another reason why the Mandelbrot set is considered to be one of the most complex of mathematical objects.

(figure 33, zoom on inversion of Mandelbrot set)

Self-similarity is one of the defining characteristics of fractals. There are other cases where fractals are intimately bound up with inversion. The simplest is to

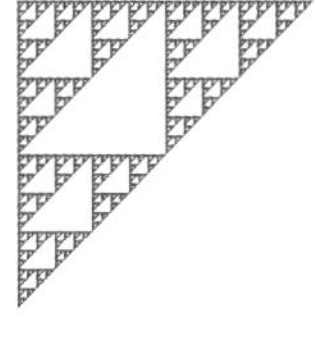 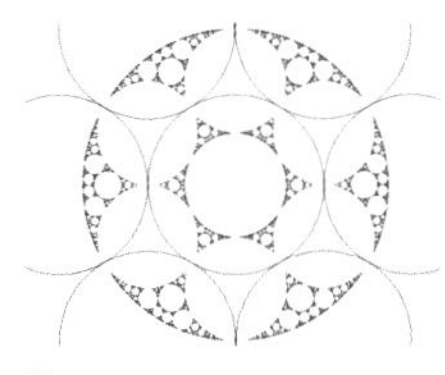 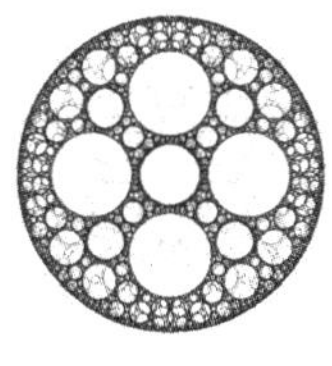

35   36   37

take a set of circles and repeatedly invert all circles in one another as they are constructed, as in figure 34.

(figure 34, fractal of circles generated by repeated inversion)

Another type of fractal is created by random iteration; one of the best-known methods is to take a triangle, choose a random starting point, select one of the points of the triangle and construct a new point halfway between them. Repeat with this new point and the result, known as a limit set, is the Sierpinski gasket.

(figure 35, Sierpinski gasket)

Limit sets produced using inversion give rise to far more complicated fractals. Take a set of circles, choose a random starting point, then randomly select a circle and invert the point, and keep on repeating the process. When the circles do not overlap, the

result has some similarity with figure 36, but the circles of the limit set are tangential and form a gasket.

(figure 36, limit set of seven circles)

When the circles do overlap, as in figure 37, the gasket becomes more complex.

(figure 37, limit set of four overlapping circles)

This process can also be carried out in three dimensions. The example shown in figure 38 is a stereo pair.

(figure 38, spatial limit set using spheres)

Below: This is a stereoscopic pair which enables you to see the surface in three dimensions. Place the page eight to nine inches from your eyes; then cross your eyes slightly so that you see three images. Focus your attention on the centre one which should appear as a three-dimensional image. This may take a few seconds, and once you can do it you should find it easier in the future.

38

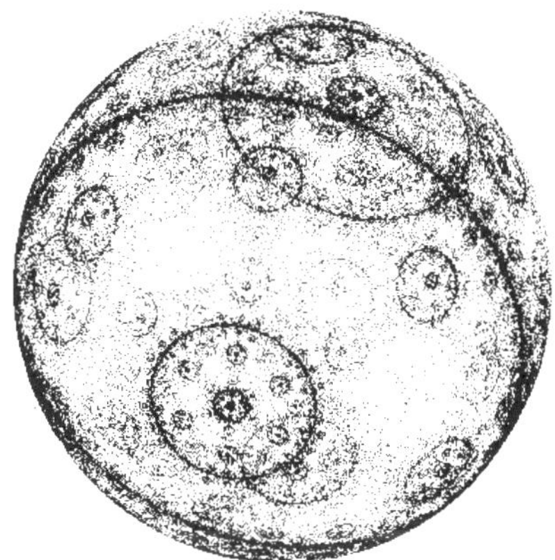 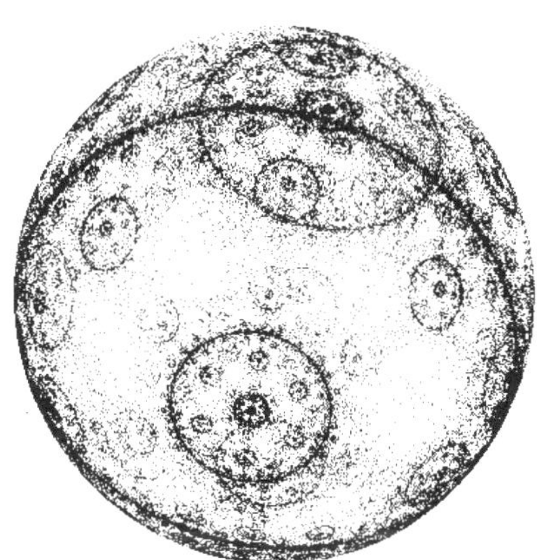

George L. Legendre is an architect and academic. He served as assistant professor at Harvard University in 1996-2000 and visiting lecturer at Princeton University in 2003-05. He has been unit master of Diploma Unit 5 at the AA since 2002. He is the author of *ijp: The Book of Surfaces* (2003) and *Bodyline* (2006), both AA Publications. In 2003 he cofounded IJP Corporation, a practice centred on the natural intersections of space, mathematics and computation. A year later IJP won the international competition for the 1000-foot-long Henderson pedestrian bridge in Singapore, currently under construction.

Mohsen Mostafavi is Dean of the College of Architecture, Art, and Planning and the Arthur L. and Isabel B. Weisenberger Professor in Architecture at Cornell University. From 1995 to 2004 he was Chairman of the Architectural Association School of Architecture, and before that Director of the Master of Architecture 1 Program at the GSD, Harvard University. His publications include *Structure as Space: Engineering and Architecture in the Works of Jürg Conzett and his Partners* (2006) and *Surface Architecture* (co-author David Leatherbarrow), which won the 2004 Bruno Zevi CICA Book Award.

John Pickering trained in classical sculpture and life drawing at Bilston and Birmingham Schools of Art. For a number of years following art school, he worked as a stone carver on projects including Saint Philip's Cathedral, Birmingham and the fifteenth-century Collegiate Church of Saint Mary, Warwick. He also worked as an assistant in a wood pattern-making factory. During the 1970s, JP shut himself off from the world and began a study of geometry which gave him access to the spatial transformations and sensual curves that have since defined his work.

John Sharp teaches geometry and art and is a regular participant in the Bridges international art and mathematics conferences. He edits *Infinity*, a new magazine on recreational and popular mathematics.

John Silver was formerly a director at Foster and Partners, where he was involved in a number of high-profile projects including the new Stansted Airport terminal building, Cambridge University Law Faculty and Commerzbank Headquarters in Frankfurt. He joined Hamilton Architects as a director in 2004.

Chris Wise is cofounder and director of Expedition Engineering and Professor of Civil Engineering Design at Imperial College, London. He holds the distinction of being the Royal Society of Arts' Royal Designer for Industry, only the second structural engineer to be honoured in this way. With Expedition Engineering and Ove Arup he has worked on numerous landmark structures including the Millennium Bridge in London, Carré d'Art in Nimes and Telecom Tower in Barcelona. He lectures, writes and broadcasts widely on creative design in engineering projects.